WHERE'S MY ENERGY GONE?

A Psychologist's Guide to Understanding Burnout, Ending the Stress Cycle and Regaining Your Sense of Control.

DR CATHERINE SYKES

Published by Zenitude Ltd®
www.zenitudeselfhelp.com

© 2021 by C M Sykes
All rights reserved.

No portion of this book may be reproduced in any form without permission from the publisher, except in the case of brief quotations embodied in critical reviews and certain other non-commercial uses permitted by copyright law.

For permissions contact:
Catherine@ drcatherinesykes.com

CONTENTS

INTRODUCTION — 5

THE EXHAUSTED TRAJECTORY — 13

PHASE 1
Motivation and Seeing the End in Your Mind — 23

PHASE 2
Understanding WHY You are Burnt Out — 43

PHASE 3
Making Changes to Stay within your Optimum Zone — 67

PHASE 4
Living in your Optimum Zone — 115

FINALLY — 119

ADDITIONAL RESOURCES — 123

INTRODUCTION

DOES EVERYTHING FEEL A BIT TOO MUCH?

Too much to do, too much communication, too much uncertainty.

In your efforts to keep up, are you multitasking, struggling to put in the required effort, assuming any failings are down to you and you alone? Do you feel that when you try to share, your problems seem minimal compared to everyone else's, leaving you feeling unheard and lonely?

Is it all getting on top of you?

Do you want a sense of control over your life? Do you want to feel as though you have the capacity to achieve your life goals?

I understand you. The world is changing at an increasingly fast pace. The problem is humans are not changing. As a practising psychologist, I have seen an unprecedented increase in clients whose mental health breakdowns and unexplained illness stories start with being too busy, overwhelmed and constantly exhausted. They have told themselves that they can handle it, or they should be able to handle it because everyone else can. They have told themselves that only lazy people can't handle the pace of modern life. But I can assure you, the vast majority are not handling it, and if we do not take steps to fix it now, being constantly exhausted will become the new normal. If you ignore all the signs of exhaustion, then your body and mind will find themselves shutting down.

With this book, I can help you to notice the signs and take the brave decision to get off what I call 'the exhausted trajectory', regaining control, mastery, purpose and energy along the way. Sometimes, people carry the fear that recovering from burnout means having to submit to a mediocre life with unreachable goals. This fear stops us from taking a good look at our lives. Unfulfilled life goals are not the result of you breaking those patterns of exhaustion. Exhaustion itself prevents you from reaching your goals. I can help you learn how to live in your optimum zone, a life where you are optimally challenged but not pushed into exhaustion and burnout. When you live in your optimum zone, you give yourself a better chance of reaching your goals. You feel more in control of your life.

HOW TO USE THIS BOOK

As you read through this book, you should make sure you have a notepad and pen handy to chart your progress. This is the perfect way to write down useful ideas and notes, and to celebrate progress whilst engaging the problem-solving parts of your brain. Having said that, many people today are dependent on electronic notes written on their phones or other devices. So, handwrite if you can, but any way of recording your responses to the questions and the exercises, as well as your general thoughts, feelings and progress, will be beneficial for you.

Your diary is a crucial part of this healing process. Using a diary to capture your own personal reflections has been shown to support the ability to make sense of your experiences. Throughout this book, I will pose questions that are an invitation for you to think about yourself and your life. This book is not intended as a place where you will find lots of facts and figures. It is intended to be like a conversation with me where I invite you to do the hard work of thinking about what is not working for you.

You will need to commit to regularly diving into the book, but the commitment needs to be manageable and sustainable. You do not need to make extensive notes, but they need to be written in a way that benefits you in the long run. Also, be realistic with your expectations regarding your diary entries. It is better to write concise notes every day than to write an essay in the first few days and then stop because it is unsustainable.

If you are new to keeping diaries or journals, it can be hard at first to get into the habit. If you have never kept one before, it is all too easy to forget to make your daily entry. For this reason, I recommend that you set yourself an alarm or reminder until you have established the habit of writing. As part of my practice as a psychologist, I often work with clients who experience burnout and unexplained illnesses. The benefits of face-to-face support and encouragement cannot be underestimated, and of course, you do not get this with a book. To compensate for this, it is a good idea to ask a family member or friend to provide support and encouragement throughout the process. Ask your chosen person to read this book beforehand and decide with them the type and frequency of support you require to ensure they are in a position to provide it.

I use many of the techniques and resources featured in this book as part of my practice. I invite you to experiment with these techniques; do not be afraid to discover what works best for you.

This easy-to-follow book will guide you through the four phases that will teach you how to end the cycle of feeling overwhelmed and exhausted. Each phase is an important step in your journey. Making any change is not easy, and as humans, we naturally go for the easiest and most familiar routes.

Phase 1 will motivate you to make the necessary changes. Phase 2 will help you understand why you are exhausted. Phase 3 will help you to make some changes. And finally, Phase 4 will help you think about maintaining your changes so you can lead your energised life with purpose. You can take all of the phases at your own pace, but in order to get the most out of the journey and enjoy long term results, you must work on all four phases.

- **PHASE 1**
  Motivation and seeing the end in your mind. The exercises here are designed for you to visualise how your life could be by replacing exhaustion with energy and purpose, and to encourage and motivate you to take action.

- **PHASE 2**
  Understanding WHY you are exhausted. This phase encourages you to reflect and identify the causes of your own personal state of exhaustion.

- **PHASE 3**

  Making changes to stay within your 'optimum zone'. This phase builds on the problems identified in Phase 2 and helps you to identify relevant changes to move from exhaustion to your 'optimum zone' which is a place where your energy levels are optimum, and you feel your life is manageable and has a purpose.

- **PHASE 4**

  Living in your optimum zone. Life can be difficult so this phase helps you to think about maintaining your changes so you can lead your energised life with purpose.

For those who feel like speed reading the book, try and avoid it. These are reflective exercises, and you need to devote a decent period of time in order to make the changes and healthier mindset stick. This book is about reflecting and putting effort into the techniques. The power of this book is really in the implementation of the techniques.

To help make this as clear as possible, there are two icons to look out for:

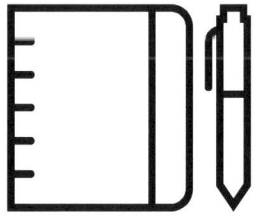

When you see this icon, it is time to PAUSE and write notes in your notebook or create a note on your phone, tablet or eBook. If you are in a busy environment, close your eyes and think about the questions before you take notes.

This icon is to let you know that it is time to set a REMINDER on your phone or on a sticky note.

THE EXHAUSTED TRAJECTORY

WE LIVE IN A BUSY WORLD WITH FEWER BOUNDARIES in a time of rapid change. On the one hand, life has improved; women have more freedoms and access to education and health care has improved. Lots of serious infectious diseases have been eradicated. Travel affords us an opening to different cultures. We can choose our entertainment at the push of a button. Yet, throughout the Western world, depression is a huge problem, and it is a growing problem. At the current rate of increase, it will soon be the second most disabling condition behind heart disease. Despite all the advances we have access to, modern life still has ways of making us feel overwhelmed, exhausted, lonely, depressed and unwell.

It was not too long ago that many boundaries were set by others. Shops, services, banks, restaurants and cafés had opening and closing times, and outside of those times, you could not be served. People accessed email from a desktop computer or a laptop, often in work time only, and rarely once they had left work. There was a social etiquette for appropriate times to make social calls. Public spaces were not for finishing business and making work calls. Cameras only came out at special events.

The further we push ourselves, the fewer the boundaries there are to contain us. We now live in a world that demands our attention 24/7. On the other side of the scale, it only takes a few clicks to meet our own demands, which does not sound too bad in itself... at first. But the reality is that our inboxes can be filled with new demands for the next day as we sleep, and this is not only from work. We can receive demands from a range of companies we rely on to live a smooth daily life, such as banks, insurance companies, phone companies and supermarkets. They all request our attention, asking us to click a few more buttons.

On one level, this gives us a sense that we have the freedom to use our time as we choose, which is an amazing advancement. However, the reality is that our day can be filled with more and more monotonous and repetitive tasks. The problem is humans love habits. Habits allow us to go on autopilot. Autopilot is easier. These monotonous, repetitive tasks soon become our autopilot.

At some level, we may gain a certain amount of satisfaction for having ticked something off our list of things to do. It can become quite addictive - we get a small release of a neurotransmitter called dopamine, which makes us feel good for having completed a task. However, over time, ticking things off our to-do list becomes the main use of our time, leaving us feeling unfulfilled and unchallenged resulting in dissatisfaction, and we find ourselves taking on new quick-fix tasks to fill our time. Social media tempts us to click and swipe and maintain the repetitive and mundane autopilot actions that we have become accustomed to. Often these quick-fix repetitive actions eat into our down-time, sleep-time, connecting-time, cooking-time, nurturing-time and even our toilet-time! It is a common misconception that people 'relax' while looking at their phones.

But it is not relaxing the brain; it is reinforcing the mundane, repetitive autopilot. Going online and using social media may seem like ways to slow down, but the constant scrolling and taking in of information just adds to brain fatigue. To relax your brain, you need less input from the outside world. If you are constantly focused on your phone, your precious down-time is being taken over by a mundane and tiring activity. We cannot achieve our long-term goals and live by our true values because there is no time left for them. Over time, this can become quite unfulfilling and then depressing as our goals and values become more and more out of reach.

With little time available for switching off, we enter a constant state of exhaustion. We feel physically tired. The brain is like a muscle that needs a resting period. Just like a muscle, it gets tired if we overuse it. Eventually it 'snaps'. It burns out. In this state we disengage, and our bodies collapse inwards as we try to shield ourselves from more demands. Suddenly, multi-tasking and everything that once felt doable requires energy we no longer possess. We do not want the stimulation of other people, so we slowly disengage, declining invitations and social gatherings and opportunities to be with others.

A lack of social support often makes people more vulnerable to poor mental health. Over time, this lonely, non-stop, lack-of-purpose way of life can lead to chronic fatigue, unexplained illnesses or prolonged recovery from illness and mental health problems.

If we get stuck in exhausted gear, daily life requires more and more effort from our mind and body. We start to feel a need to rush. However, our bodies and minds are not made to be constantly

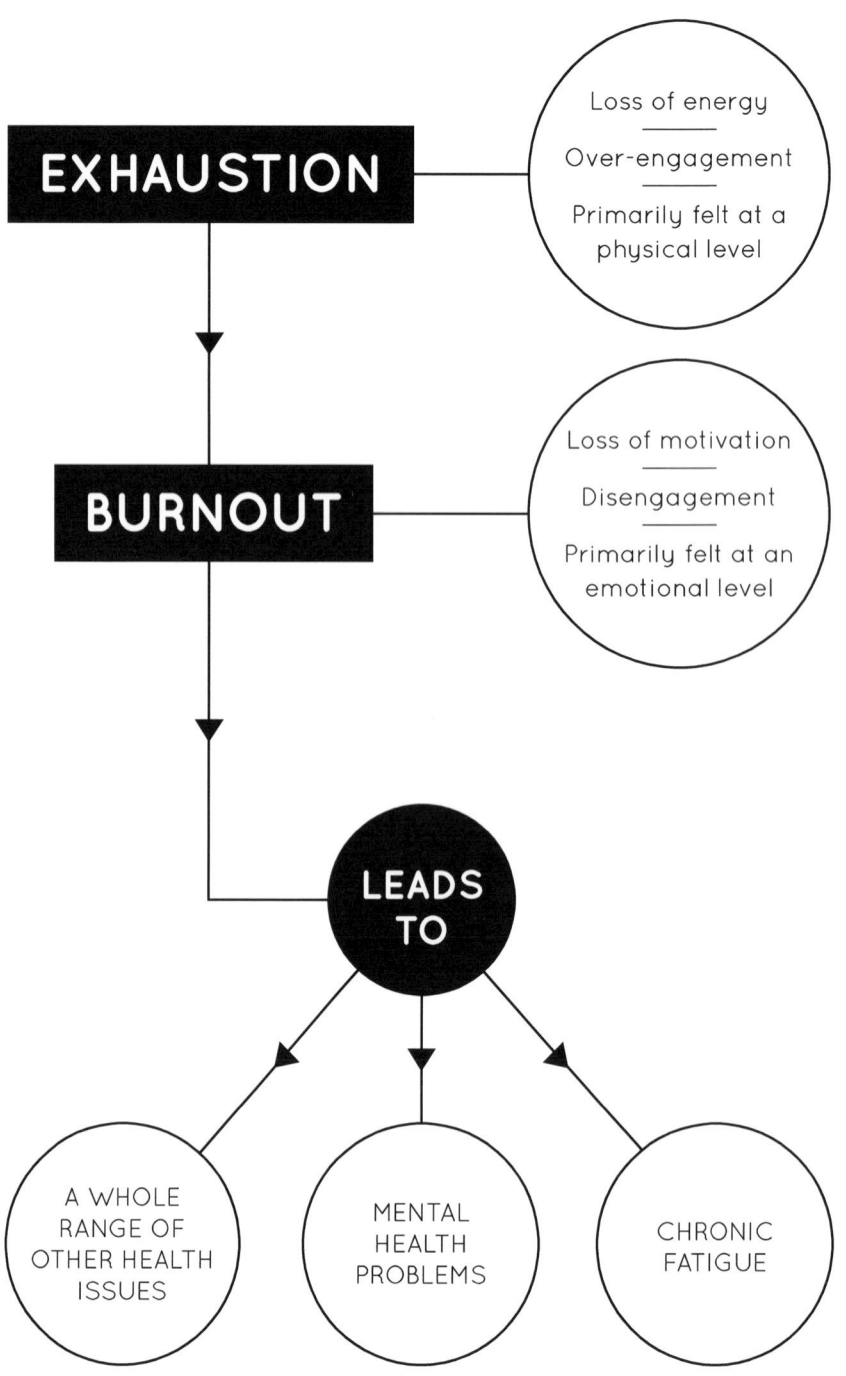

rushing. We start to interpret our rushing as never having enough time. This struggle with time has psychological consequences. It can cause chronic anger, depression, bitterness, resentment, and even sudden hopelessness.

Why does feeling exhausted and rushing lead to being sick and tired all the time?

Psychologists have determined that it is not necessarily stress that is bad for us. Kelly McGonigal explains that if we attach meaning to our stress, we are less likely to be impacted by it. In other words, there is a personal sense of purpose attached to the stress that you are under. For example, if you are working hard to get a business off the ground and you are clear about why you are setting up the business and believe in your strengths to set up the business, then that meaning you have attached to activities can protect you to a certain degree from the harmful factors of stress as long as it is combined with regular periods of rest and ideally a focus on the sense of satisfaction and pride from the achievements towards the goal.

However, many people do not attach meaningful purpose to their stress and, let's face it, it is hard to attach meaning to mundane repetitive tasks. Many people do not stop and take in the sense of achievement and pride in the process of achieving goals. The focus is only on the end goal. This means that you are more likely to be overwhelmed and exhausted by stress. Instead of stopping and re-evaluating what is being done and why, most people have a tendency to push and push, set more unrealistic goals, fuel their bodies with caffeine and sugar, and sometimes alcohol or drugs, to induce a switch-off. At the same time, it is common to engage in critical self-talk, such as, 'I should be able to do this, everyone else can do it', which only adds more pressure to the body and mind. This puts pressure on the mind and body and causes an overload which is experienced as exhaustion and feeling overwhelmed. To be precise this state of constant exhaustion and feeling overwhelmed causes an allostatic overload. Allostatic load is a measure of 'wear and tear' on the body.

Our bodily systems are ideally designed to cope with stress in the short term. All our internal organs know exactly what to do. There is a cascade of physiological responses to help us deal with immediate stress. In particular, the adrenal glands release adrenaline and cortisol, which are hormones that help the body get through difficult situations. When adrenaline is released, your heart rate and breathing speed up. Cortisol sends glucose and protein from stores in your liver into the blood. This makes energy immediately available to your muscles to prepare your body to either 'fight' the stress or 'flee' from the stress.

However, when the body systems that are activated to help us deal with stress work too hard for too long, the body slowly breaks down in different ways. Too much cortisol becomes toxic for the body and over time, the body starts to suppress non-emergency functions, such as digestion and reproduction. If the cortisol sticks around, it suppresses the immune system. Cortisol is part of the body's complex natural alarm system which also communicates with the brain regions that control mood, motivation and fear. Some experts have named stress as the greatest proxy killer, as the impact of what it does to the body can be deadly over time.

Our body expects us to turn off the physiological responses to stress. The physiological responses are not designed to cope with the long-term ongoing stress of disharmony, uncertainty and imbalance. Over time, there is an increased physiological arousal to deal with stress, which overloads the body's systems and causes an overload of the body's allostatic load or 'wear and tear' response. This is experienced as physical and mental illness.

Another important consideration in understanding the bodily impact of stress is the vagus nerve. The vagus nerve is the longest and most complex of the twelve cranial nerves that extend from the brain to our chest. It is made up of fibres that primarily link the brain stem to the lungs, heart, and gut, but also reaches and interacts strongly with the liver, kidneys, spleen, gallbladder, ureter, female fertility organs, neck, ears, and tongue. The vagus nerve controls the parasympathetic nervous system, intervening in many functions from digestion to heart rate, to perspiration.

As it is so long and wandering (vagus literally means wandering in Latin), it controls and affects many parts of our conscious and unconscious bodily functions, such as maintaining a constant heart rate, digesting food, and breathing, as well as the parts that process and manage emotions.

When activated, the vagus nerve has a calming effect on bodily functions. Some of the vagus nerve functions in our body are:

- Helping regulate our heartbeat, controlling muscle movements and maintaining the pace of breathing.

- Maintaining the functioning of the digestive tract, allowing the contraction of the stomach and intestine muscles to digest food.

- Facilitating relaxation after a stressful situation.

- Sending sensory information to the brain about organ status.

Therefore, dysfunction of the vagus nerve can lead to mood swings and other ills, such as seizures, B12 deficiencies, and obesity. Mental and emotional stress can inflame the nerve, along with fatigue and anxiety. Our posture can impact on the function of the vagus nerve. If we close our body inwards and reduce eye contact, then the functioning of the vagus nerve can be impacted. Therefore, strengthening the function of the vagus nerve can improve conditions, such as exhaustion.

A higher vagal tone is connected with lowered anxiety levels, improved mood, and greater resilience to stress overall.

The below actions help to increase the vagal tone:

- Slow, deep breathing from the diaphragm.

- Humming or repeating the sound 'OM'.

- Splashing cold water on your face.

Another issue that is contributing to exhaustion is the increase in multiple things demanding our attention. Today's modern world has increased the possibility of multitasking. This may seem like it improves our productivity, but in reality, multitasking slows down our efficiency. It takes longer to complete tasks when we multi-task. The brain has evolved to focus on one thing at a time. These days, we demand our brain to cope with more stimuli than it is physically or mentally capable of, putting the brain under stress. This means that we are less focused and take longer to complete tasks. This sense of frustration can lead to rushing and carrying on using our brain's capacity into the evening and night when the body is preparing physiologically to sleep. By fighting your body's natural rhythm, you put extra strain on an already tired body and mind. If you continue this lifestyle pattern, over time you begin to notice the psychological and physiological impact.

So, by now, you should have some insights into what being exhausted and rushing all the time can do to your mind and body. You will discover more as you work through this book. Right now, you may feel powerless to change. Phase 1 helps you to start to think about what change might look like so as to motivate you to start to make some changes.

PHASE 1

Motivation and Seeing the End in your Mind

TIME TO START JOTTING DOWN NOTES. PUT SOME time aside and find a safe space to sit down and ask yourself some important questions. Do not feel like you have to commit hours upon hours. The more time you feel you have to put aside for asking questions, the longer you will have to wait for satisfactory answers. And do not ask yourself these questions when you are in the middle of a busy task and you have got a range of questions competing for your attention. Commit around fifteen minutes of relaxed and focused time. However long it takes, try and tackle it within fifteen minute chunks. This is a good balancing act, giving you just enough time to give the questions some serious thought, but not so long that you are putting other stuff on the back-burner.

At the end of this book there is a free resource to test how burnout may be impacting your cognitive abilities. The test is fun and quick to use, it has been developed by scientists at Cambridge University, UK. Once you start to make some changes, you can go back to the test to see if the changes you are making are improving your Attention and Mental Concentration.

Discover your optimum self.

You may be way out of your optimum zone right now. I want to help you recognise how you got out of it. Performing out of your optimum zone can at first be exhilarating. It feels like you are achieving so much. I'm afraid if you stay out of your optimum zone for too long, it is a slippery slope down into burnout and for some, eventually a breakdown. The problem is, once you are in burnout or breakdown, it is a harder ladder to climb back you to your optimum zone.

Learning to ask questions about yourself is a powerful way to start finding inspiration to live the life you really want and which is in tune with your authentic self. Asking questions cuts through the mental fog and gives clarity to help you climb back into your optimum zone and regain your sense of control.

Take a look at the optimum zone graph to the right. It demonstrates the relationship between performance and stress. This is a general guide to how our performance will vary depending on the different levels of stress. We all have an optimum amount of stress/demands/stimulation that keeps us in a peak performance state. If you fear that taking your foot off the pedal will lead to a mediocre life or that you will loose your job or fail in life, then please take a look at this graph. When we discover and stay longer in our optimum zone, there is actually an increase in performance. If you are constantly exhausted, this impacts your performance and you move further away from having the energy and time for your goals.

Throughout this book, I want to help you to discover and understand your optimum zone and stay in it for longer periods of time. When you are in this state, you are better able to live a life with purpose, feel more balanced and live in an energised body.

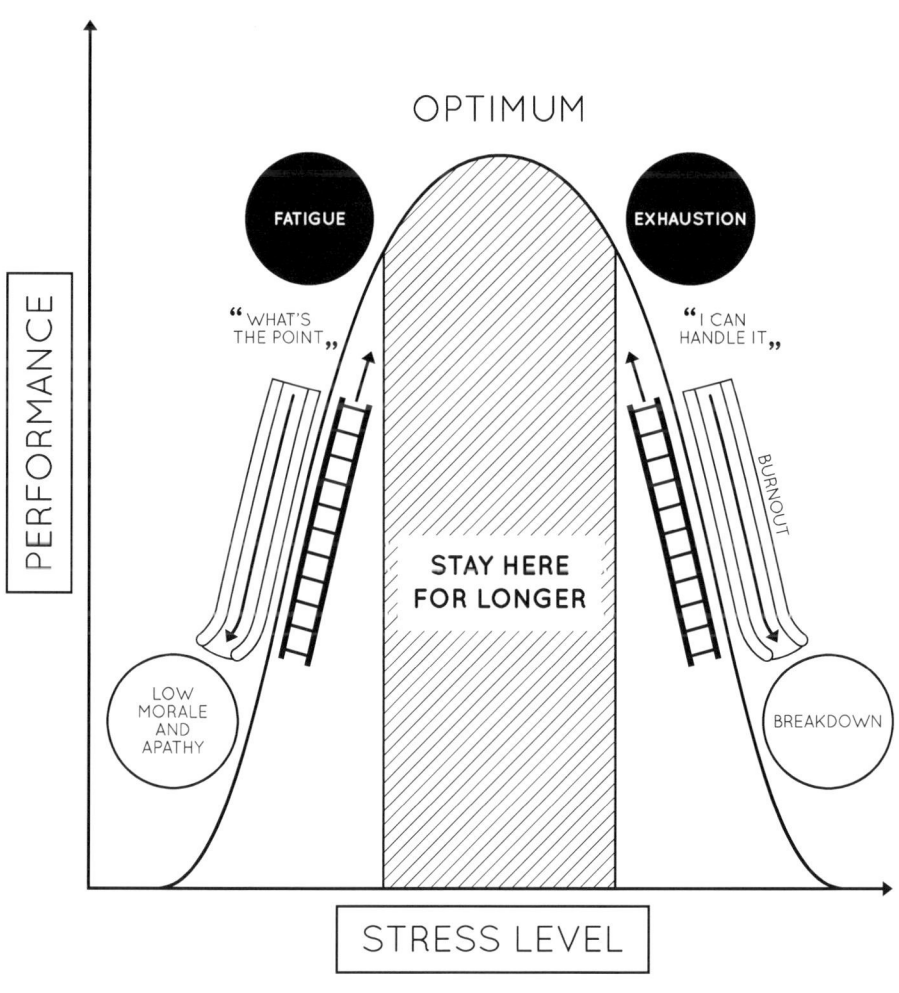

Let me explain the optimum zone graph with a simple example. If we are performing repetitive tasks that require little concentration, for example, washing up after a boring week at work, we might be at the bottom left of the graph. We might be bored with low morale. The same would apply if we were asked to write our signature one hundred times. However, if we were asked to write with our non-natural hand, we would need to concentrate to perform well and we would have been optimally challenged to learn a new skill. Imagine then, that you are doing this exercise with a time limit hanging over you. You would either complete the task with terrible signatures or produce fewer than one hundred good signatures. Either way, we would be at the bottom right of the graph, under great stress and under-performing.

This example is just a simple analogy of a one-off task but imagine this high-stress level being a constant presence in your life. We would slide from optimum performance to exhaustion. If we had to keep repeating this task our motivation to learn the new skill would drop. If we kept trying under the same conditions, our enthusiasm for the task would wane and rather than give up slowly, it would feel like a quick slide down into burnout. If we kept on telling ourselves 'I should be able to do this' "Only lazy people stop', or 'people need to me to do this' and continued with the task without thinking of a way around it, asking for help or questioning if people really need you to do the task, then you would end up breaking down. Exhaustion to burnout then to breakdown is like a quick slippery slide. However, getting back into the optimum zone following the subsequent burnout and breakdown is trying to get a footing on a steep ladder and we need to take it one step at a time. I have structured this book in a way to help you to choose the best steps for you in order for you to change. I understand that you may be keen to start to make some changes, but I strongly advise you not to rush up the ladder.

EXHAUSTION AND FATIGUE

Fatigue is a state where you might be under-stimulated and feeling tired, not because of over activity but because of under activity. It's a kind of numb shutdown. This can happen in weekly phases or longer periods. A weekly phase may be when someone is constantly exhausted and too busy during the weekdays then crashes into fatigue at the weekend, staying in bed too long, not seeing people, ordering take-away food, and generally being too tired to take care of themselves. Others have longer periods of exhaustion and are busy during the weekdays and weekends, before gradually slowing down and crashing into the fatigued zone as their bodies try to signal 'slow down'.

Living between these two extremes - exhaustion and fatigue – takes quite a toll on the bodily systems, often resulting in physical health problems. This pattern can be quite scary and depressing. You may feel that your body is letting you down. You may become anxious as your body may feel unpredictable and out of control. You may feel frustrated about this pattern and not understand it. Your interpretation of your bodily experience may lead to mental health problems as you become anxious about what is happening to you.

In order to make changes, we need to understand what we are trying to achieve. I want you to start a process of discovering, understanding or remembering what it means to be at your optimum self. But firstly, let's tune in to the exhausted zone as this might be more familiar at the moment. Do you constantly feel tired? Are you always ill? Do you feel down and unmotivated? Clear your mind and dwell for a moment on the unrest in your life.

Then review the following questions while making notes:

- What are you doing that causes these feelings?

- What are you NOT doing that you would like to be doing?

- What are you thinking when you are in this exhausted state? Start to observe and make notes on your thoughts.

- Quite often, people think something along the lines of, "I can handle it.'

- What emotions do you feel?

- What does your body feel like?

- How many hours are you sleeping?

- Is anything/anyone interrupting your sleep?

- Describe your diet to yourself.

Ask yourself the same questions for the fatigued zone and how you experience it. Before moving on, just take a few minutes to focus on those negative feelings and thoughts.

Next, let's try to tune into when you felt good, for example, feeling more energetic, healthy, happy and motivated. If this is still difficult for you, don't worry. Take your time. Recall some periods or moments when everything felt optimum, for example, passing a driving test or an important exam, falling in love or holding hands with your child on a beach. Focus on a period when you felt you could manage life... anything that represented an optimum moment. Dwell on that feeling for a while then ask yourself the following questions. Do not worry if you find a question too difficult, just go to the next one.

In your recollection of an optimum time:

- How would you describe yourself when you are at your optimum when life feels balanced and manageable?

- What are you doing?

- What are you feeling?

- How are others behaving when they are around you?

- How many hours are you sleeping?

- Is anything/anyone interrupting your sleep?

- Describe your diet in this period.

Now, let's move to some further self-discovery questions:

- What makes you smile?

- What do you like about yourself?

- What mistakes have you learnt from?

- What hardships have you overcome? How did you cope? What did you have to do to adapt?

- What emotions and bodily sensations do you want to experience as you move through each day?

- How do you want to be remembered?

- When was the last time you felt at your optimum?

Before moving on, just take a few minutes to focus on those optimum feelings.

This exercise aims to help you start with the end goal in mind, so you know why you are taking the necessary steps to make changes in your life so that you can spend longer periods in the optimum zone.

Now you need to make a commitment to observe and record moments when you feel good, no matter how fleeting the feeling. Then pause and acknowledge what you are thinking about, what you are doing, and what you are thinking when you feel that way. This is an ongoing process of self-discovery, as what makes you feel good will change through the course of your life. Right now, you may be in a new phase of life, requiring you to rediscover what feels good. This may feel daunting at first, like an upward struggle to climb back into your optimum zone. Sliding out of it was probably much easier and more automatic. However, to continue full engagement with life, we must be prepared to face our fears and continue to explore ourselves and life.

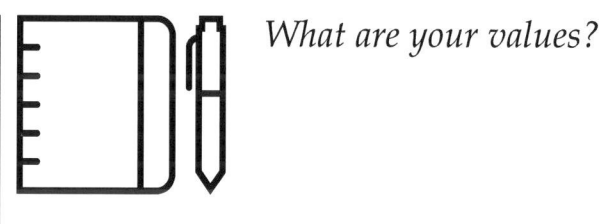

What are your values?

To help you understand what living in your optimum zone feels like, it would be useful to start a process of tuning into your values. Values are your deepest wishes for how you want to behave as a human being. Values are not about what you want to obtain or achieve; they are about who you are and how you want to behave or act on an ongoing basis. Understanding why you are busy or why you want to make changes to your lifestyle is pivotal. Having a purpose makes it easier to endure difficulty or make difficult changes.

There are hundreds of different values, and below you will find a list of some common ones suggested by Russ Harris, the author of 'The Happiness Trap'. Whilst these are good values to have, you must focus on your individual values and which ones resonate with the idealised version of yourself. There are no such things as 'right' or 'wrong' values. Similarly, your values may differ from another person's values.

So, read through the list overleaf and write a letter next to each value: V = very important, Q = quite important, and N = not so important. Try to score about ten of them as very important. Some people find this exercise difficult as they find that all of the values are important. All of the values are important but try to focus on what is really very important to you personally.

- [✓] **ACCEPTANCE:** to be open to and accepting of myself, others, life, etc.

- [ ] **ADVENTURE:** to be adventurous; to actively seek, create, or explore novel or stimulating experiences.

- [ ] **ASSERTIVENESS:** to respectfully stand up for my rights and request what I want.

- [✓] **AUTHENTICITY:** to be authentic, genuine, and real; to be true to myself.

- [ ] **BEAUTY:** to appreciate, create, nurture, or cultivate beauty in myself, others, the environment, etc.

- [ ] **CARING:** to be caring towards myself, others, the environment, etc.

- [ ] **CHALLENGE:** to keep challenging myself to grow, learn and improve.

- [ ] **COMPASSION:** to act with kindness towards those who are suffering.

- [✓] **CONNECTION:** to engage fully in whatever I am doing and be fully present with others.

- [ ] **CONTRIBUTION:** to contribute, help, assist, or make a positive difference to myself or others.

☐ **CONFORMITY:** to be respectful of and obedient towards rules and obligations.

☐ **COOPERATION:** to be cooperative and collaborative with others.

☐ **COURAGE:** to be courageous or brave; to persist in the face of fear, threat or difficulty.

☐ **CREATIVITY:** to be creative or innovative.

☐ **CURIOSITY:** to be curious, open-minded, and interested; to explore and discover.

☐ **ENCOURAGEMENT:** to encourage and reward behaviour that I value in myself and others.

☐ **EQUALITY:** to treat others as equal to myself, and vice-versa.

☐ **EXCITEMENT:** to seek, create, and engage in activities that are exciting, stimulating or thrilling.

☐ **FAIRNESS:** to be fair to myself and others.

☐ **FITNESS:** to maintain or improve my fitness; to look after my physical and mental health and wellbeing.

☐ **FLEXIBILITY:** to adjust and adapt readily to changing circumstances.

- [x] **FREEDOM:** to live freely; to choose how I live and behave and help others to do likewise.

- [ ] **FRIENDLINESS:** to be friendly, companionable and agreeable towards others.

- [ ] **FORGIVENESS:** to be forgiving towards myself and others.

- [ ] **FUN:** to be fun-loving; to seek, create and engage in fun-filled activities.

- [ ] **GENEROSITY:** to be generous, sharing and giving to myself and others.

- [ ] **GRATITUDE:** to be grateful for, and appreciative of, the positive aspects of myself, others and life.

- [ ] **HONESTY:** to be honest, truthful and sincere with myself and others.

- [ ] **HUMOUR:** to see and appreciate the humorous side of life.

- [ ] **HUMILITY:** to be humble or modest; to let my achievements speak for themselves.

- [ ] **INDUSTRY:** to be industrious, hard-working and dedicated.

- [ ] **INDEPENDENCE:** to be self-supportive and choose my own way of doing things.

☐ **INTIMACY:** to open up, reveal and share myself - emotionally or physically - in personal relationships.

☐ **JUSTICE:** to uphold justice and fairness.

☐ **KINDNESS:** to be kind, compassionate, considerate, nurturing and caring towards myself and others.

☐ **LOVE:** to act lovingly or affectionately towards myself and others.

☐ **MINDFULNESS:** to be conscious of, open to, and curious about my here-and-now experience.

☐ **ORDER:** to be orderly and organised.

☐ **OPEN-MINDEDNESS:** to think things through and see things from the perspective of others'.

☐ **PATIENCE:** to wait calmly for what I want.

☐ **PERSISTENCE:** to continue resolutely, despite problems or difficulties.

☐ **POWER:** to strongly influence or wield authority over others e.g., taking charge, leading or organising.

☐ **RECIPROCITY:** to build relationships in which there is a fair balance of giving and taking.

☐ **RESPECT:** to be respectful towards myself or others; to be polite, considerate and to show positive regard.

☐ **RESPONSIBILITY:** to be responsible and accountable for my actions.

☐ **ROMANCE:** to be romantic; to display and express love or strong affection.

☐ **SAFETY:** to secure, protect or ensure the safety of myself and others.

☐ **SELF-AWARENESS:** to be aware of my own thoughts, feelings and actions.

☐ **SELF-CARE:** to look after my health and wellbeing and ensure my needs are met.

☐ **SELF-DEVELOPMENT:** to keep growing and improving in knowledge, skills and character.

☐ **SELF-CONTROL:** to act in accordance with my own ideals.

☐ **SENSUALITY:** to create, explore and enjoy experiences that stimulate the five senses.

☐ **SEXUALITY:** to explore or express my sexuality.

☐ **SPIRITUALITY:** to connect with things bigger than myself.

☐ **SKILFULNESS:** to continually practise and improve my skills and apply myself fully when using them.

☐ **SUPPORTIVENESS:** to be supportive, helpful and encouraging, and available to myself or others.

☐ **TRUST:** to be trustworthy; to be loyal, faithful, sincere and reliable.

Insert your own unlisted value(s) here:

☐

☐

☐

☐

☐

☐

☐

Once you have marked each value as V, Q, or N, go through all the Vs and select the top six that are the most important to you. Don't worry if currently your life is not fully aligned to your values. We are just trying to understand what is important at this stage. Finally, write down these values in your notebook on the first pages. For example, if you want to be flexible but worry that your lifestyle is too rigid, do not worry. Think of it as a challenge to overcome.

Set a reminder in your phone to remind you of your six values on a daily basis for one month, then every other day for the next month, then weekly for a month, then finally set a reminder of your values for once a month.

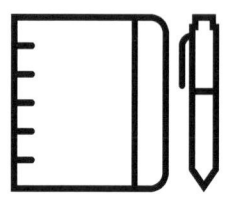

Once you have discovered more about yourself, you can start to visualise yourself in your optimum state, living life according to your values.

Imagine the physical sensations you would feel if this vision became a reality. List the feelings you would expect from your vision.

Using your notes, try to create a symbol of this positive, balanced future in your mind. The type of symbol you choose is personal and could be a visual image, word(s), or even a sound. It should include images of the end vision, but also images of the process of getting to the end vision. Try to visualise, hear, and engage with your meaningful symbol as regularly as possible. This will quickly prime your mind to focus on what you do want. Our minds like images of what we want, to make change a little easier.

> *Set a reminder to take time every day to direct your focus onto your symbol and practise the quick and simple exercise described below:*

1. Take several energetic breaths while imagining your symbol for your future. Focusing on your breathing does not need to be complicated or stressful. Just pause and become aware of your breathing. Close your eyes if you wish. What words would you use to describe your breathing? What movement do you need to take to give that breath just a little more energy? This might take some time to practise. Tuning into the symbol of your positive, balanced self should help your breathing to feel more energetic. Become familiar with this energetic sensation, even if you can only hold it for a few seconds. With practice, you will be able to hold this energetic breath for longer.

2. Try to stay with your symbol of your future for 15 - 20 seconds.

3. Plan a point in your day when you can tune into this future self. Where will you be when you access this image?

Making time to focus on this symbol of your future is an important and motivating step towards making it a reality. Set a reminder on your phone or in your diary to tune into and connect to your future self and your meaningful symbol every day.

To enhance your visualisation process, you can print an image to stick at the front of your notebook, add a photo to the notes section on your phone, or use the photo as a screen saver. Some people also like to create a secret board on Pinterest with images of all the stages of progress towards their vision.

Congratulations! You have officially taken the first step to ending your cycle of stress and burnout. With an exercise like this, it is easy to worry that you are very far away from your idealised version of yourself. But before this exercise, you may not have had a solid idea of what your idealised self would look like. You might not have known how much you value reciprocity as an example and can see yourself looking to moments where you are building meaningful relationships based on that value. Hold tight, this is an important phase of the journey of change, knowing and sensing your direction and destination. I hope knowing where you want to be gives you reason to move onto the next phase.

PHASE 2

Understanding WHY you are Burnt Out

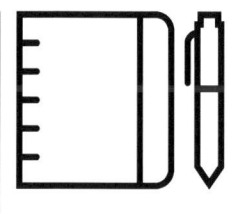

During this phase, we are going to try to understand why you are burnt out. It is going to take some time to make notes. You may think you know what the causes are for your constant exhaustion - perhaps work, children, partner, daily commutes, traffic, money issues, etc. - but prepare to be surprised. There are internal causes of exhaustion too. Let's start the process of self-discovery.

ARE YOU FAMILIAR WITH THE ROLE YOU PLAY IN exhausting yourself? Do you perceive yourself as having control over your own life? Or do you mainly blame outside sources for always feeling exhausted? Resilient people tend to have what psychologists call an internal locus of control; they believe that the actions they take will affect the outcome of an event. Of course, some factors are simply outside of our personal control, such as natural disasters and pandemics.

Whilst we may be able to put some blame on external causes, we need to feel as if we have the power to make choices that will affect our situation, our ability to cope, and our future. This sense of power can be energising and can make you take different life choices. During this phase, you need to start the process of accurately assessing what is exhausting you and wearing you down physically and mentally.

START TO NOTICE YOUR PATTERNS

To help you with this assessment, you will need to understand some basic psychology. There is an interaction between our thoughts, emotions, actions, and our bodily experiences and the way we hold our bodies. So, the way that you think impacts on how you feel emotionally, the way that you feel emotionally impacts on your thoughts. Your emotions impact your body, and your body impacts your emotions, which in turn feeds back into how you think and what actions you will take. Your actions or behaviours impact your body, emotions and thoughts. These interactions are constant and impact how we manage life, our aspirations, our health and daily life. In this phase, you are going to start to develop some insights into the interactions of your thoughts, emotions, actions and your body to help you to understand why you are exhausted and burnt out.

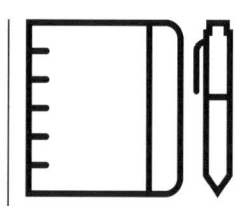

Notice your exhausted thoughts and behaviour.

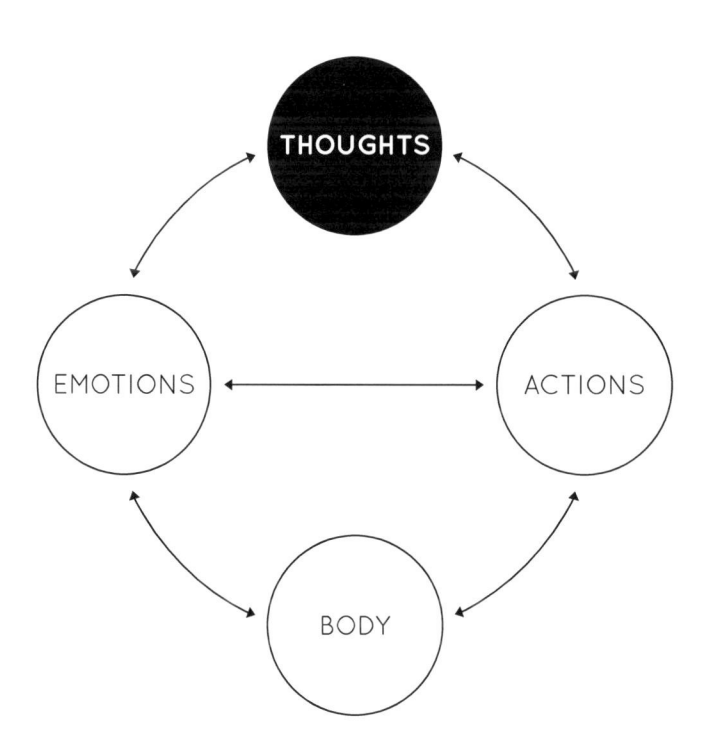

```
         THOUGHTS
        ↙       ↘
  EMOTIONS ←→ ACTIONS
        ↘       ↙
           BODY
```

Your thoughts create your reality. Consider how often you say or think:

- I'm exhausted.

- I'm tired.

- I'm so busy.

- I can't cope.

The problem with this type of thinking is that it is not often said in an observational manner, but rather the tone is often one of frustration and helplessness which can result in draining emotions like guilt, irritability, sadness, worry and shame. Carrying these emotions around impacts on your body and your posture. These emotions and the impact on the body then impact the actions we take.

For example, if you keep saying to yourself, 'Oh, I'm so exhausted' using a helpless tone, you may feel irritated with life in general, your body will feel increasingly heavy the more you keep telling yourself how tired you are. You may feel like the best action to take is to flop down helplessly into the chair, withdraw from social contact more and more, and tell yourself you are too tired to exercise on a regular basis. Over time you may create a lifestyle in which you are under-stimulated. Go back to the optimum zone graph and see the bottom left-hand corner, where people tend to experience fatigue, low morale and apathy.

Compare this when using a more curious matter-of-fact observational tone You may notice 'Oh, I'm tired' may lead to more empowering decisions, such as having an early night, moving a deadline, cancelling an arrangement, taking a relaxing bath, or making a nourishing meal. Some people are worried about taking empowering actions as they think it will make them lazy. But the reality is if you take empowering steps and listen to your body, you end up with more energy to create the life you want in the long run.

Start to become aware of how many times you use such phrases using a frustrated and helpless tone. If you have someone supporting you through this process, ask them to point out when you are talking about your exhausted state with frustration. Keep a tally of how often you talk about your state of mind and body with frustration. Start to notice what you do if the tone you use is more curious and observational.

ARE YOU LIVING IN YOUR BODY OR YOUR HEAD?

By paying attention to how your body feels, you are tapping into a wealth of information and wisdom about your health. There is an important relationship between how you think, what you do, and how your body feels. By listening to your body and making notes in your diary, you will start to notice objective patterns between your behaviour and your sensations of tiredness. This may feel strange at first as many people are not used to really living in their body. Their experience of living mainly comes from a sense of being in their head, especially for people with a perfectionist mindset. Their head rules their existence. Perfectionism has become a way to feel safe but a perfectionist thinking style takes its toll on your body.

Perfectionism is an unrealistic goal to strive for and can take its toll on you both mentally and physically. It can lead to isolation and disappointment and make you prone to getting unwell and tired. Perfectionism primes relationships to fail. Quite often, perfectionist thinkers engage in self-talk along the lines of, 'No one can do things as well as I can.' They don't 'suffer fools.' They become easily disappointed in relationships, and other people tend to find themselves preferring not to spend time with them.

This can cause major problems, as feeling safe with others lowers the heart rate, relaxes the muscles and sends positive signals to the nervous system, which in turn helps to relieve stress and take the edge off modern living.

People with a tendency towards perfectionism tend to engage in 'all or nothing' thinking. Therefore, their feelings about a certain situation will fall at one of two extreme ends of a spectrum. They have either succeeded totally or failed entirely. A task or activity either went perfectly or it was a disaster. Everything has to be or look a certain way. This swaying between two extremes of emotions can be exhausting at a physical level and mental level.

Consider for a moment, you are a perfectionist taking an exam. You have completed most of the questions, then you arrive at a problem that you know you have revised but cannot remember the solution to. Your time is up, but you have still not answered that one question. Therefore, you consider yourself a failure, overlooking the fact that your overall performance on the paper was very good. How might this feel like to be constantly in a state of self-doubt?

Just as personality can be a factor in contributing to constantly feeling exhausted, it can also be a perpetuating factor. People with a tendency towards perfectionism may be particularly prone to falling into unhelpful ways of managing exhaustion. Perfectionist personalities are more likely to find it difficult to take breaks and rests during the day, as they feel they are 'wasting time' and should be doing 'something useful'. However, planning a healthy level of rest into the day is not wasting time at all. Instead, it is a vital part of managing your mind and body so you can continue to enjoy activities in ways that are sustainable.

Perfectionism usually stems from an unhelpful deep-rooted belief about yourself, such as 'I'm unlovable', 'I'm not worthy', 'I'm not good enough' or 'I'm second best'. You may not be aware of these beliefs, but they drive your thinking style and behaviour. People engage in perfectionism as a way to hide these deep beliefs. The problem is people can have difficulty confronting the reality that they cannot be 100% perfect 100% all the time. When you are in a situation where you cannot be perfect, this can cause anxiety or a low mood as you evaluate the situation in accordance with your unhelpful deep beliefs about yourself. After some time, you start to think that the way forward is to perfect your perfectionism - in other words, you need to be better at being perfect. Over time, you put unrealistic demands upon yourself and your everyday state becomes one of exhaustion. This is what psychologists' call, The Perfectionist Trap.

Make a note of any extreme language you personally use, such as, 'Never', 'Always', 'Totally', 'Total disaster', 'There was no point at all' or 'What a total waste of time'.

If this sounds like you, do not worry. Simply be aware that you have this pattern of thinking as you progress through the book. Try to notice if you fall into perfectionist thinking so you can begin to challenge some of your less helpful beliefs, especially around rest. Make notes about where in your life you tend to apply perfectionist thinking. This can manifest in the forms of work, parenting, relationships, appearances or housework. Sometimes perfectionists find it hard to accept that they are perfectionists as they do not see themselves as perfect in all areas of life. Someone may be a perfectionist at work but have a messy home, for example. This type of person finds it hard to accept that they may have a perfectionist style of thinking.

ARE YOU DOING ENOUGH TO NOURISH YOUR BODY?

One of the first basic forms of self-care you relinquish when exhaustion sets in is eating well. Healthy eating requires time and planning. You think you do not have time when you are feeling rushed and exhausted. Rather than work at preparing a healthy meal or snack, you find yourself bingeing on the most immediately accessible foods, such as chocolate bars. But eating well can protect you from stress. Ask yourself the following questions - and you may be surprised by the results:

WHAT DO YOU EAT WHEN YOU ARE EXHAUSTED?

If you are not familiar with the foods you reach for when you are exhausted, start to pay attention to what you are eating and make a list. I have worked with many people who almost go into a trance-like state when they start eating due to exhaustion. They can literally forget what they have eaten.

HOW DO YOU JUSTIFY THAT WHAT YOU EAT IS FINE?

For example, do you promise to eat better tomorrow? Do you focus on one healthy ingredient and ignore the other ingredients? I once had a case in which a client justified eating crisps (potato chips) as OK because a potato was a vegetable. I have worked with many clients who eat a diet full of healthy greens during the daytime but by the evening they are craving sugar and will overeat sweet treats. Despite this regular pattern of overeating sugar, they still identified themselves with being a healthy eater.

HOW DO YOU FEEL AFTER YOU HAVE EATEN?

Do you rush your food without allowing your mind and body to acknowledge that it has eaten? If you have reached a point that you are rushing every meal, then you start to feel that everything you do has a deadline to it. This is a very stressful state to be in. Constant time pressures make you feel helpless.

ARE YOU DRINKING ENOUGH WATER?

We get more dehydrated when we are under stress because the heart rate goes up and we breathe more heavily, so we lose more fluid.

Research suggests that losing as little as 1% of your body weight in fluid may reduce mental performance, as well as potentially inducing fatigue and headache. This mild level of dehydration can easily occur over the course of a normal day's activities, which highlights how important drinking little and often is to stay within your optimum zone.

Each individual's needs are unique to them and depend on their health, age, size and weight, as well as activity levels. Generally speaking, a woman should aim to drink about 1.6 litres and a man should aim for 2 litres

It may seem too simple to think about which substances are impacting your energy levels, but you should not ignore the simple observations. Ask yourself what your typical habits are when it comes to nourishing your body, and then jot down any thoughts in your notebook.

IS YOUR PERCEPTION OF TIME, CORRECT?

Do you try to stretch time by overcommitting and convincing yourself that you have plenty of time?

Do you get frustrated and anger with yourself if you don't manage everything on your list of things to do?

Do you find that it is actually very difficult for you to measure time? Somehow your brain cannot plan ahead.

What kind of person do you think it makes you if you take time to plan and accurately assess your time?

In my experience, I have found that people who burnout out have lots of unhelpful beliefs about time and planning. People either try to over control time and put too much energy into trying to control time. They get exhausted and stressed about time. Others think that planning is for boring people. They avoid planning and tell themselves that they like to go with the flow. Both of these extreme time-related thoughts and behaviours are not productive and often lead to a lot of stress. This is because our brains have different capacities when it comes to planning and some of us are not natural planners. People who have difficulty in planning may justify it to themselves as 'it's just the way I am' or 'I'm a more spontaneous kind of a person'. While I do not want to suggest that we all need to be the same type of person, I do want to help people who struggle with planning to accept that planning is difficult and that it may be holding them back, and to accept that they may need to put some planning systems in place when it comes to managing time and using time more purposefully and get what they need from life.

To stay in the optimum zone of productivity, you need to start to be more balanced about time and use it more deliberately and flexibly. To help you do this, you need to get the maths of the day right. Then you can move towards taking deliberate action to use your time more purposefully.

I am going to help you to take the first steps towards using your time more intentionally.

Stress results when our demands outweigh our capacity. We need to think of time in terms of it being a capacity factor. We all have 24 hours in our day. Time has become the most precious currency in modern life. It can be quite stressful trying to fit in so many demands and expectations into one day. In order to cope, we rush around trying to gain a few more seconds here and there. The end result is that we are not really present in the activities that we are trying to fit in. There are just rushed versions of ourselves moving through the day. This existence can result in memory difficulties as it takes time to encode experience to memory, especially positive memories. We encode negative experience almost immediately, but it takes 12 seconds to encode positive memories. If we are rushing our experiences, they do not get encoded to memory properly. This results in other problems, such as a loss of confidence, more time needed to carry out tasks as we have not got the full experience to draw upon to repeat tasks or forgetfulness which results in tasks taking longer.

It is common to engage in self-critical thoughts when you forget something, such as, 'I can't believe I forgot.' 'How stupid!' 'Loser!' Or 'You silly person, what have you done?' Your mind and body listen to these messages which are basically another way of saying, 'You can't cope in the world'. So, you go around with a sense that life is hard, and you can't cope. This can result in you putting tension into your body, trying harder, putting more demands upon yourself, or retreating by doing less, and hunching your body inwards to protect it from the world. Muscle tension is a reflex reaction to stress. It is the body's way of guarding against injury and pain.

To obtain what you want from life, you need to understand the basic maths of your day and start to use your time more deliberately. Choose how you want to use your time instead of spending most of your time on autopilot. Assess accurately how much time you have available. What is your capacity? We need to get the maths of your day right to help you to get off the exhausted trajectory.

We must all carry out some basic functions to stay alive, such as sleeping, eating and drinking, personal care and caring for our home. People often try to rush or skip these basic functions in the race against time. I have heard people say that 'sleep is for weak people'. 'If I were strong enough, I should be able to survive on one meal a day'. I know people in senior positions who say they don't have time to take a shower every day. In this exercise, assess how much time you really need for these basic tasks that keep us alive and functioning. There are other tasks that we have to carry out too, such as working and studying, commuting and travelling, childcare, family member care and socialising.

Let's do the maths for your day. You can do this as an average per day or, if it makes more sense, you can break it down by weekdays and weekends:

STEP 1:
What is X?

Write a list of all your basic functions. Then allocate an amount of time for each function. Then add up that time. This is your X.

Example:

- Winding down and sleeping = **8 hours**

- Eating and drinking = **1 hour 30 minutes**
  (includes shopping, cooking, buying food from shops, cafés, canteens, restaurants, washing up, etc.)

- Showering, getting dressed, self-care = **45 minutes**

- Care for the home = **30 minutes**

- X = **11 hours and 15 minutes**.

STEP 2:
What is Y?

Write a list of all your non-negotiable tasks that you have to carry out. Then allocate an amount of time for each task. Then add up that time. This is your Y.

Example:

- Work = **8 hours**

- Travel = **1 hour**

- Childcare = **2 hours and 45 minutes**

- Y = **11 hours and 45 minutes**.

Then add X + Y. This gives you your Z.

Based on the X and Y examples above Z = **23 hours**.

Quite often, there is barely any time left. Let's find out your A or what I like to call your *Activation Energy*, the time you actually have for all those other demands of your time and for what you really hope to get out of your life.

Your A can be calculated by subtracting your Z from 24 (the number of hours in each day).

Based on the X, Y and Z examples above A = **1 hour**.

A gives you an accurate idea of how much time you have left for all of the other things you would like from life. Having this figure in mind helps you to accurately assess if you have the capacity to accept all the extra demands you put on yourself, or all the other demands that others put on you. It also helps you to figure when you do have the time to start to take small steps to include activities that will take you one step closer to leading the life you want. You may find that as you pay attention to this time and commit to using it for meaningful activities, you have more time for this meaningful activity. For example, I have written this book gradually using 2 available hours a week because I want to help more people deal with burnout. I started with making half an hour available each week.

Having in mind how much time you really have available also makes taking time for B *(Balancing Time)* more doable. *Balancing Time* is when you protect moments throughout the day to purposely switch off your brain. I suggest 5 x 2 minutes of non-negotiable, full switch-off time a day. It was only a few years ago that I used to suggest 15 minutes of *Balancing Time* to my clients, but I have noticed that 15 minutes has become difficult for lots of people, so I now suggest 5 x 2 minutes.

This may not seem a lot, but you will be surprised how many people do not even manage this. You may also be surprised how energising it is to purposefully take small amounts of guilt-free, fully present, *Balancing Time*.

Most people do not have a great deal of *Activation Energy* during the week, especially if they are working and/or caring for others, so *Activation Energy* and *Balancing Time* needs to be treated and used like a precious resource that it is.

An example of how you might use your precious *Activation Energy* and *Balancing Time*:

- **5 minutes** of yoga in the morning.

- **10 minutes** of daily exercise.

- **10 minutes** of proper switch-off time (5 x 2 minutes).

- **15 minutes** of call/contact with important family and friends.

- **10 minutes** of reading about something new and interesting.

- **10 minutes** of making a step towards a life goal (e.g., internet searching, reading a book, making notes, writing the plan).

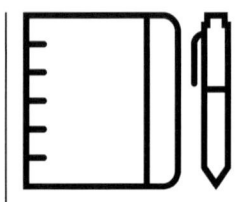

Now for some reflection.

How much time do you currently have for your *Activation Energy*, that precious time to take steps towards the life you want to lead? How are you currently using this precious time?

Are you happy with how your *Activation Energy* is being used? How much proper *Balancing Time* do you get per day, time to reduce input and switch off?

What gets in the way of you taking *Balancing Time*?

Do you feel guilty if you take time to pause? Do you think you will let your guard down and then will not be able to achieve all the other things you need to do? Make a note of your thoughts about taking *Balancing Time*. Stand back from these thoughts and evaluate them with the knowledge that taking time to pause, taking a step towards your life goals, will ultimately make you feel energised and less stressed.

The key to ensuring you actually use this precious Time is to set aside time in your schedule to make it happen. Get in the habit of thinking about your *Activation Energy* time in units of minutes. Tell yourself, 'I am now switching modes; I am about to go into *Activation Energy* mode.' We are not very good at switching between different types of actions, so we need to pre-warn ourselves that we need a different type of mental energy.

Now, I am a realist. I know that this will not go according to plan all the time. If it does not, please do not start a spiral of self-criticism that convinces you to stop altogether. Accept it has not happened then think about the next slot you have to use your *Activation Energy*. You are creating small steps and may make more time in the future for these activities.

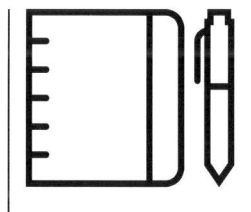

Do you know your drainers and energisers?

Have you noticed what and who either drains your energy or energises you? Do you have too many unfinished projects, unread books, cupboards that need tidying, or clothes and gadgets you never use? Does a friend, family member or a colleague put too many demands on you? All of this clutter can slowly drain your energy by taking up too much mental space and chipping away at your everyday focus. Similarly, there are certain objects, activities and people that can give us energy. Make a list of your drainers and energisers in your notebook or on your phone.

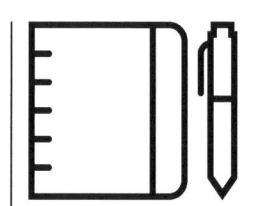

Does your sleep pattern deplete you?

For many people who feel exhausted and who are regularly unwell, getting good quality and undisturbed sleep can feel like an uphill struggle. Sometimes we let ourselves slip into unhealthy sleeping patterns over a period of time, and it is important to look at whether improving your sleep routine may be helpful to feel more energised.

Having irregular bedtimes, getting up at different times each day, resting excessively during the daytime, or waking up worrying, can all make it harder to fall asleep and stay asleep at night. This can lead to shortened sleep or can cause your sleep to be disturbed. Therefore, you are unlikely to feel refreshed when you wake in the morning.

Make a note of your sleep patterns.

- What time do you go to sleep?

- What are you doing before you go to sleep? Does it feel relaxing?

- How long does it take you to go to sleep?
  Do you wake up during the night? How many times?

- Do you worry at night? Do you try to solve problems at night?

- Are you comfortable in bed?

- Do you snooze your alarm clock? If so, how many times?

- Do you get frustrated about not sleeping? Make a note of your thoughts about not sleeping.

- Do you worry about the next day if you cannot sleep?

- Make a note of your worries about not sleeping.

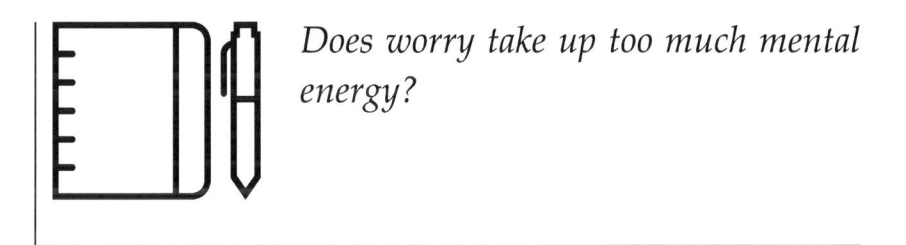

Does worry take up too much mental energy?

Worry is something we do. It is part of our basic human nature to worry. It is also one of the most exhausting traits we possess. Worries, doubts and anxieties are a normal part of life. It is natural to worry about an unpaid bill, an upcoming job interview, or a first date. But 'normal' worry becomes excessive when it is persistent and uncontrollable. If you worry every day about 'what-ifs' and worst-case scenarios, or you cannot get anxious thoughts out of your head, it interferes with your daily life. It can slow you down, cause sleep problems, and ultimately keep you exhausted.

Constant worrying, negative thinking and always expecting the worst can take a toll on your emotional and physical health. It can sap your emotional strength, leaving you feeling restless and jumpy. It can also cause headaches, stomach problems and muscle tension, making it difficult to concentrate. You may take your negative feelings out on the people closest to you, self-medicate with alcohol or drugs, or try to distract yourself by zoning out in front of screens.

If you are plagued by exaggerated worry and tension, there are steps you can take to turn off anxious thoughts, or at the very least, keep them at bay. Chronic worrying is a mental habit that can be broken. You can train your brain to stay calm and look at life from a more balanced, less fearful and therefore less reluctant perspective. But before you learn how to deal with worries, I want you to first assess why it may be hard for you to stop worrying. Some beliefs about worry only fuel existing worry and keep you in a never-ending cycle of worry and exhaustion.

NEGATIVE BELIEFS ABOUT WORRY

You may believe that your constant worrying is harmful or that it is going to have a negative impact on your mental health or affect your physical health. You may worry that you are going to lose all control over your worrying; that it will take over and never stop. This may make you avoid thinking about issues in your life that need problem-solving. I assure you that even if you think you are doing well to ignore an issue, at some level, if that issue is unresolved, it will be taking up mental space and energy and slowing you down. It may also be taking up physical space in your body. No matter what we do, unresolved worries will always find a way to gain our attention and hinder our lives.

While negative beliefs, or worrying about worrying, add to your anxiety and keeps worry going, positive beliefs about worrying can be just as damaging.

POSITIVE BELIEFS ABOUT WORRY

You may believe that your worrying helps you avoid bad things, prevents problems, prepares you for the worst, or leads to solutions. Maybe you tell yourself that if you keep worrying about a problem long enough, you will eventually be able to figure it out? Or perhaps you are convinced that worrying is a responsible thing to do, or the only way to ensure you do not overlook something, convincing yourself that worrying about someone is a sign of love and care. If you believe that your worrying serves a positive purpose, then you will find it even more difficult to break the habit. Once you realise that worrying is the problem, not the solution, you can regain control of your worried mind.

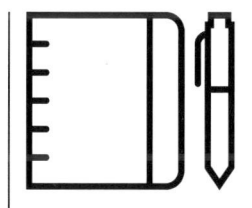

Do you hold any negative or positive beliefs about worry?

I would like you to make some time, again 15 minutes of focused time in the first instance, longer if possible, to get out your notes and start to list all the worries you have. Try to be as specific as possible.

DO YOU ACKNOWLEDGE THE EXTERNAL FACTORS THAT CONTRIBUTE TOWARDS YOUR EXHAUSTION?

So far, this book has focused on what you can do to take control of your exhaustion. However, it is important to acknowledge that there are some external factors that add to the constant sense of exhaustion. Economic, environmental, geographical, health and workplace culture all contribute towards exhaustion. It is beyond the scope of this book to address all of these factors of life. But the first step in the right direction is acknowledging that there are some factors that are beyond your control and you need to shift your focus to the factors you can influence. I briefly mention this here so that you can bear in mind any related negative or self- blame thoughts.

Total self-blame thoughts include:

- What is wrong with me?

- Why can't I just..?

- I'm so lazy.

Total power to external factors include:

- Life sucks.

- It's alright for some.

- I just can't.

- I'll never be able to...

- People like me don't get to...

- If I slip up at work, I'll get fired.

Start to pay attention to these types of thoughts. Note them down and start to be curious about how much power they take away from you.

Well done, you have reached an important part of the journey. When we force ourselves to look at factors that we cannot control, it is not uncommon to feel a sense of hopelessness. But Phase 2 is intended to be an enlightening phase that offers you a sense of awareness about what you can and cannot control in your life and give you the push to focus on what you can control in life and by extension, make room for the things you want in your life.

PHASE 3

Making Changes to Stay within your Optimum Zone

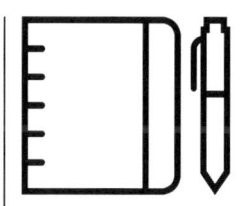

> *Find time to sit somewhere quiet and ask yourself, 'What have I noticed from my diary so far?' Write down your observations.*

YOU DO NOT NEED TO JUMP INTO MAKING CHANGES all at once. Read the following techniques, then at the end of this phase, plan where you are going to start. At the end of this phase, you will be asking yourself what seems the most realistic change that you need to make first?

As you are reading phase 3, make a list of what you are noticing is a contributing problem to your burnout then as you get inspired, write a list of the solutions you need to take. Once you have acknowledged what the problem is, you may find other solutions not mentioned in this book. You may come up with your own ideas or find ideas from other sources of advice. For now though, just keep reading then at the end you can plan in more detail what and when you want to make changes.

You will have better chances of success and implementing these life lessons if you have someone on hand to help you. Working with a psychologist would help to pace you through your changes and support you to take realistic and incremental steps, working through any setbacks with you along the way. Alternatively, talking through your plan of change with someone you trust would help to give you some perspective on the realistic nature of your plan. Also, it usually helps to enhance your commitment to change once you have shared it with someone out loud.

As we move into this phase, we will be focusing on reframing your thought patterns and changing your behaviour to start making positive changes to your routine. Make sure you keep your diary on hand throughout this process. It is important to keep monitoring your energy levels throughout the process so you can spot patterns and figure out what works for you. None of the techniques are stand-alone techniques that are going to work in isolation. To make improvements to your energy levels, you really need to have done the diary work to understand what is going on for you and what you need.

DEALING WITH UNHELPFUL THINKING PATTERNS ABOUT EXHAUSTION

It may sound simplistic to notice and rethink your thoughts about exhaustion. You may ask, 'How can something so simple help me?' You may feel outraged by the suggestion of something so simple. Well, it looks simple on paper but the practice of noticing your thoughts and rethinking them repetitively is not simple. It takes patience, insight and effort.

Because we have been accustomed to a particular way of thinking, the new ways of thinking may not seem real at all and therefore difficult to implement, but I urge you to give it some time. For some people, if they do not get instant results from an exercise, they feel inclined to give up and move on. But think of it like working out. You are unlikely to develop muscles after one exercise. It is a long and sometimes draining process but the long-term results will make it all worth it. To encourage you to continue, please pay attention to how you feel when you start to change your way of thinking.

Quite often, my clients get stuck on the following self-critical thoughts:

- Why am I so exhausted?

- Why me?

- Why can't I cope?

- Why not her/him?

- Why can't I fix this?

- Why is everyone else coping?

Do you hear yourself saying these things? If so, notice the tone, is it a kind or helpful voice? Probably not. It is more likely to be harsh, cold or angry. Your first instinct is to feel frustrated at things that seem constantly out of your control and you may hold yourself responsible. Thinking about who that voice reminds you of can be quite motivating in wanting to change that voice.

Next time you hear that harsh, cold or angry tone as you think about your exhaustion, ask yourself, 'Does the voice remind me of anyone in my past who was critical of me?' Write the name of that voice in your notebook. My critical voice belongs to...

It can be an emotional experience as you run through these self-critical thoughts. But it can be quite revealing if those thoughts belong to someone in your past, and you are finding the previously unknown source for your self-doubt. As you notice and name the person to whom those thoughts belong, take a deep calming breath to stabilise yourself. Repeat this over and over until you feel emotionally grounded. Once you feel a sense of stabilisation, try to experiment with more compassionate thoughts. Here are some examples; see if any of the below bring a sense of calm and clarity.

Examples of compassionate thoughts:

- Being human means being imperfect. Everyone has some sort of painful experience.

- My body is not my enemy. We are on the same team.

- Why not me? Humans get sick and tired.

- Feeling overwhelmed all the time is not a sign of weakness. It is a signal that something needs to change.

- I can choose to take a new and healthy action.

- I don't need to rush. I can slow down my pace and still be as effective.

- Look at what I've done right today.

You will notice that compassionate thoughts are more soothing and gentler, and if you have worked yourself into a habit of constantly doubting yourself, it is a welcome change of pace. Commit to noticing those self-critical thoughts, taking a deep breath and replacing those thoughts with more compassionate thoughts. Being more self-compassionate will not make you lazy or more likely to fail. Quite the opposite, you are more likely to find the energy to pace yourself to achieve what you need to achieve and to find more clarity and solutions to your problems. We are all taught about the importance of kindness. But self-kindness is an important trait in helping you help others and recognising the positive qualities of yourself.

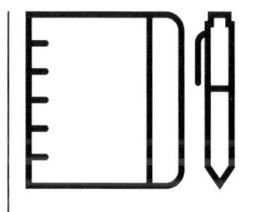

As you read these alternative thoughts, do you notice a sign of relief? What happens to your body?

GET OUT OF THE PERFECTIONIST TRAP

If perfectionism is part of your personality, approach this aspect with understanding and compassion. Even though we all have unique personalities, perfectionism is a trait shared by many people. However, it is important to be mindful of your perfectionist streak and to take the steps to actively challenge it. Otherwise, perfectionist thoughts will drive you to continue with intense activity or overdo your solution/cure seeking and avoid rest, because your mind is focused on being productive.

We seldom look at rest as an appropriate thing, however, when we've had adequate rest, we are enabled to do things to a better degree and gain a greater sense of emotional fulfilment and knowledge that we are doing the best we can rather than struggle through a task.

Perfectionist thinking can derail your efforts to make positive changes, such as following a diet or exercise regime, or in this case, establishing healthy new thought patterns and routines. If you don't feel you have performed perfectly, you may feel you have failed entirely, and this can cause you to become demotivated and give up or, for some, to frantically search for the next new method.

The solution to this is to try to look at the 'bigger picture' to gain a more realistic and compassionate perspective on what you are really achieving. It is easy to become fixated on all the things that have gone wrong. The drawback of the perfectionist mindset is the feeling that if we have not gotten anything right, we might as well have gotten nothing right. But that is not the case. You forget that it is possible to achieve to get things right, but they get pushed to the side of your brain. Give yourself permission to do things 'well enough' instead of perfectly is a kinder and more realistic way of managing your life.

I have four helpful suggestions for how you can begin to manage perfectionist thinking and find a more balanced way of thinking.

1. THE 80/20 RULE

An interesting and useful concept when dealing with

perfectionism is the 80/20 rule or Pareto's rule. Pareto was an Italian economist who observed that 80% of land belonged to the wealthiest 20% of people. He then explored this further and discovered that the 80/20 rule applied to a wide variety of situations. It follows that 20% of your activities will lead to 80% of your productivity. In other words, this is a way of prioritising your activities to make your load more manageable.

Try writing out your 'to do' list in your diary. Do not just include chores or work-related tasks. This is stuff that you HAVE to do, but your diary is a personal reflection of you and that should be reflected in how you plan your day. Therefore, you need to include leisure and social activities that bring you joy.

Taking part in pleasurable activities will improve your mood and sense of wellbeing, and you deserve to make these a priority. Now, try writing these out in order of importance and mark out the top 20%. Try focusing on accomplishing the top 20% instead of getting bogged down in the 80% that are less vital. This will make your list of activities less overwhelming and will ensure that you are expending your limited energy on the things that matter most.

It may seem to you that there are items in your 80% that are still very important. One problem you may have is feeling that you have to take on all of these issues alone, which can lead to the feeling that you are taking on the world single-handedly. But there are people in your life who can help you share the burden. Could you ask for help from family, friends or colleagues to accomplish these tasks to leave you free to focus on your top 20%? Think about who can take on these tasks? Do you have a child who is growing up and could take on extra responsibility?

Do you have a friend that you can call on? Is there someone in your team who would gladly take on extra responsibility? When was the last time you or your partner assessed the division of labour? Does this need a revision? Does the task need to be done now; can you schedule it later in the diary? Is there another way to do tasks with similar results? By sharing the task, your world will feel much less isolated.

2. URGENT AND IMPORTANT ACTIVITIES

Good time management means being effective as well as efficient. In other words, we must spend time on activities that are important and not just urgent. To help you assess what is important and what is urgent, make sure you understand the difference.

- **Important** activities lead to us achieving our goals, whether these are professional or personal. Life goals are commonly listed as important because they resonate with what we want to achieve as an individual and also may take more time to achieve (some may even take years). Some can be social engagement, such as mixing with friends and giving you a chance to expand your social circle. Depending on the life you lead, these can be important based on how infrequently they appear. But these are ultimately emotionally rewarding activities.

- **Urgent** activities demand immediate attention. They are often associated with achieving someone else's goals, which means if we carry out the task, we are going to get an immediate hit of satisfaction or relief from pleasing others or giving in to others. They grab our attention. We often go onto autopilot in dealing with these activities, which at some level is easier than deliberately turning our attention to an activity that has a longer-term gratification.

When we know which activities are important and which are urgent, we can overcome our natural tendency to automatically respond to unimportant urgent activities and forget important/not urgent tasks. This increases our chances of having enough time to align our activities to our values. In doing so, life becomes more pleasurable and energising. Use an urgent/important matrix when you write your list of things to do. Be sure to plan time for your important/not urgent activities. These are the activities that you are more likely to get a buzz out of.

3. AIM FOR EXCELLENCE AS OPPOSED TO PERFECTION

Many people see excellence and perfection as the same thing. But in reality, aiming for excellence in what you do is far more healthy, productive and rewarding than striving for perfection. So, how do the two differ?

Essentially, perfection is an unattainable standard that we aim for out of fear of not being good enough. When we fail to achieve this unreachable goal, the result is self-criticism and a sense of failure. Perfection means getting things right 100% of the time and achieving 100% of all what we set out to do, which is a feat so unmanageable that even those with boundless energy would fail. Not helping this feeling is if you are prone to comparing yourself by the merits of other people. We have all been in situations where we look at what other people have in terms of relationships or jobs, and always find ourselves feeling a pang of self-doubt if we are not living the life we think they are leading. Sometimes, we see value in certain things because society says we should. When you think about who you want to be and what you want in life, try to purposefully take your focus to the things that matter to you. Go back to your values to help you with this focus.

Excellence, however, means striving to do the best that you can do in your daily activities. It involves focusing on the tasks that really matter and aiming to get them done to a high standard, but not to an unrealistically perfect standard. This is an achievable and aspirational aim and will be far better for your self-esteem and sense of achievement than constantly chasing perfection. If you apply Pareto's 80/20 rule, the aim of reaching excellence is a good fit. This means that in the time it would take you to try to carry out one task to complete perfection, you could achieve several other goals to an excellent standard in the same time-frame. Shifting your thinking with regard to what is an acceptable standard will free up your time and allow you to achieve more personally meaningful goals while expending less energy. Essentially, you are making all the right moves towards the life you want to have and that is the most important thing.

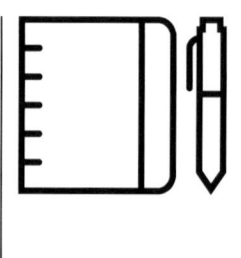

Think about how you use your time. Pick one thing you do to perfection and make a goal to do it to an excellent standard instead. What do you need to change? What do you need to stop doing? What do you need to stop thinking? What will be the worst

> *thing that would happen if you made some changes?*

4. AIM TO DIFFERENTIATE YOURSELF

It is often wrongly assumed that we will have more career success through working hard and delivering without pause. In today's world of work, being busy is not going to give you the edge, because everyone around you is busy. You need to differentiate yourself. If you are stuck in a job where you are trying hard to be better than others, let me tell you a secret. 'Better' is a flimsy mirage. It keeps you locked in the same ways of working as everyone else. 'Better' is temporary as someone can always come along and be better than you. You somehow know this deep-down, and it keeps you on guard and uncomfortable which either causes added stress as you add more demands to compete which pushes you out of your optimum zone, or it makes you resigned where you do not quite take yourself to your full potential and you stay out of your optimum zone, in the fatigued, low morale zone.

Focusing on the details can lead to an overwhelming sense of being constantly busy, and more prone to exhaustion. We give ourselves more to do, instead of giving ourselves time to really think about the opportunities and solutions available to us. This strong need to feel useful, and the desire to appear hardworking, offers a convenient escape from taking a step back to really evaluate the problem. It is easier to engage in safe, mundane, busy tasks than tackle the more complex mental and emotional work.

Instead, walk your own path. You do not want to follow the sheep that stay together. You're an individual. Resist the pressure to conform to the 'demand avalanche' and have the confidence to do your own thing, to differentiate yourself as someone who allows themselves the time to properly think through the 'big stuff' that will really make a difference. It is time to move on from 'more, more, more'. Instead, it is time to:

- **Learn to focus** - it is easy to get distracted in today's world. To focus you need to avoid the temptation of 'busy' and 'quick fixes'. It is in focusing on a task, that you can get better at it. You get better at a task then you can develop your expertise in the task. Clutter has no place when you are striving for excellence.

- **Prioritise** - set up good routines to align your values with your day. Do what is most important before all else.

- **Problem-solving** - moaning about your problems takes energy. Use this energy to think creatively about how you can solve your problems. Ask yourself, 'Is there another way to do this?' Use the worry tree to let go of the energy it takes to worry.

Tapping into yourself and believing more strongly in your own capabilities generates perspective and creates self-confidence. You become sure of yourself which increases the likelihood of doing new and difficult things. That leap of faith that once seemed scary and daunting instead feels like a challenge you are ready to take. Differentiating yourself as a person who thinks this way, instead of allowing busyness to overwhelm and exhaust you, can only lead to success. Less really is more.

The first step to differentiating yourself is to acknowledge your key strengths. Below are some strengths to help you to start to think about your key strengths. Notice that responding quickly and keeping everyone happy is not on the list! That is because you need to focus on your inner self before you can turn the focus to your surroundings. Choose your top 10 strengths. Think about how these top strengths can help you in your life and career. Think about how you want to use these strengths to your advantage to enable you to lead the life you want.

Now, think about what your top strength in your work life is. Then, think about how you can best use this top strength in your work life.

Sincere	Wise	Thoughtful
Calm	Organised	Creative
Patient	Positive	Generous
Determined	Dependable	Resilient
Appreciative	Engaging	Insightful
Warm	Humorous	Caring
Focused	Brave	Fair
Strategic	Rigorous	Independent
Understanding	Detailed	Hopeful
Open-minded	Practical	Playful
Curious	Supportive	Decisive

DEALING WITH DRAINERS AND ENERGISERS

Get to know what energises you. Factor these energisers into your *Balancing Time*. Start to make a list of activities, people and environments that you notice energise you on a daily, weekly, monthly and yearly basis. Make a commitment to yourself to include more energisers in your life.

It could be an activity like walking a dog or doing something with a friend. But it does not just energise you, it also makes you feel more complete. Similarly, make a plan to make some small adjustments to gradually reduce the drainers from your life and bring in more of your energisers.

Examples of rapid energisers:

- Stand up and stretch.

- Drink cold water.

- Go outside and look up at the sky.

- Listen/hum/dance to a feel-good song.

- Have a laugh with a friend.

- Tickle a loved one.

- Breathe deeply.

- Read out loud something inspiring.

ENERGISERS

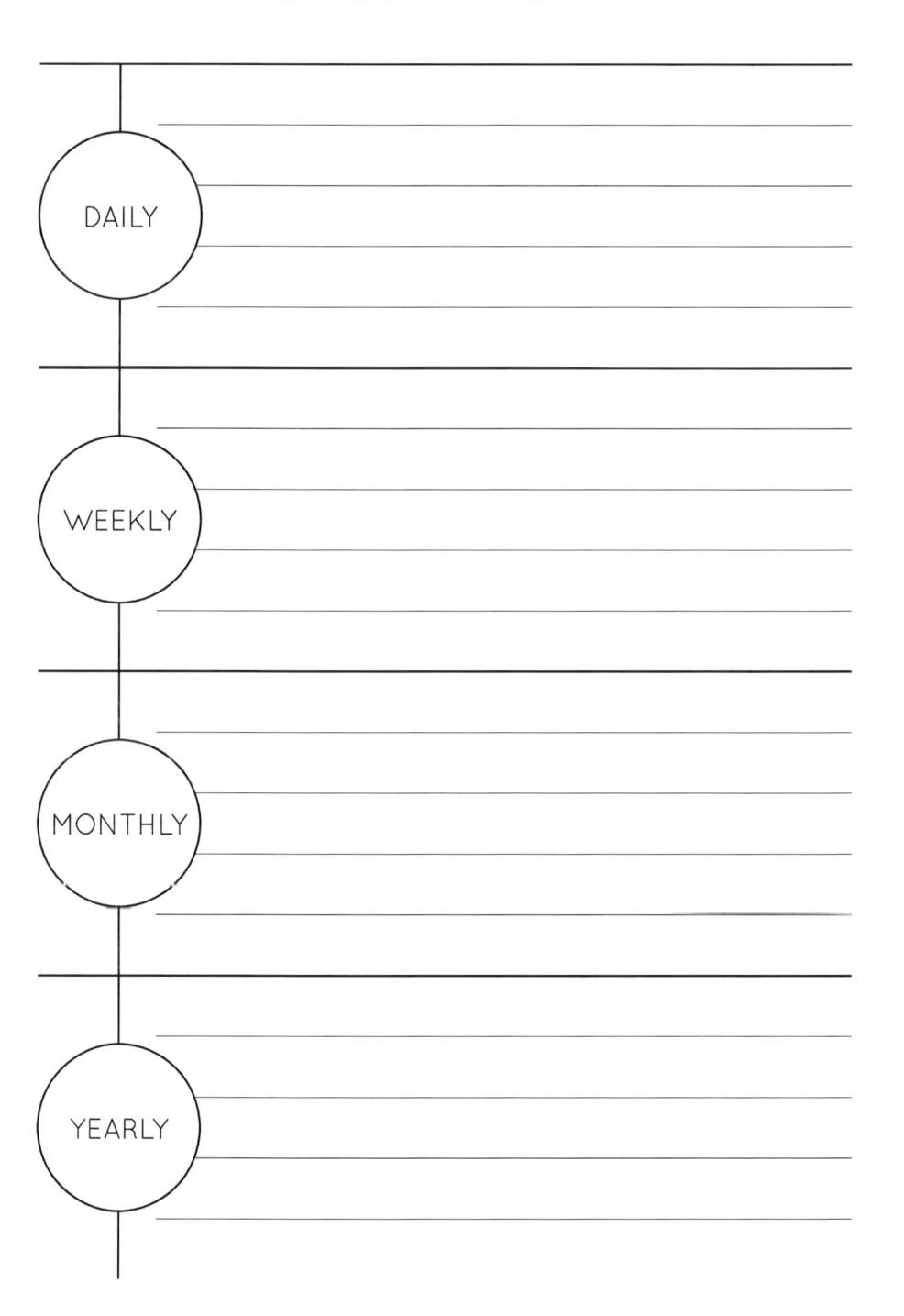

- DAILY

- WEEKLY

- MONTHLY

- YEARLY

- Five minutes of yoga.

- Read a few pages from a good book.

- Get some fresh air and Vitamin D.

- Tend to plants or flowers.

- Change into comfortable or smart clothes.

- Sip green tea.

- Cuddle a pet.

- Draw or paint.

- Take a walk outside in nature.

- Eat a slow-release, low GI snack, such as peanut butter on sliced apple.

- Take a shower and use an invigorating shower gel and body lotion.

- Sit up straight - shifting your posture can immediately give you more energy.

It is a good idea to build regular energisers into your life on a daily, weekly, monthly and even yearly basis. Think about what your energisers could be. What could get in the way of making these energisers happen? Could they be practical points or thinking barriers? What could you do to reframe your thinking and prioritise building energisers into your life for the benefit of your physical and emotional health?

Practical barrier example:

> *I can't afford a babysitter.*

Brainstorm a solution to this problem. Could you ask a friend to look after your child(ren) and come to an arrangement to take it in turns in the future?

Thinking barrier example:

> *Taking time for myself is too indulgent.*

Rethink and reframe. You are worth some self-care. Consider the long-term impact if you do not take care of yourself.

What free time do you have spare? What could you do to energise yourself in that time?

Use the diagram overleaf to help you create a list of energisers you want to build into your life and the steps you could take to make sure they happen.

DEALING WITH DRAINING PEOPLE

Quite often people understand that boundaries are important, but they don't really know what having clear boundaries means or how to establish clear boundaries. Put simply, boundaries are stop signals and border controls that are designed to protect yourself, so it is clear that you own your life. You develop boundaries to enable you to make good choices.

There are different types of boundaries, such as physical, sexual, spiritual, relationship, emotional and mental. Here, I want to talk to you about developing your relationship and emotional boundaries with people who try to control you and drain your energy. In Phase 2, you should have gained an awareness of people who are draining you. I now want you to think about what these people are doing to drain you. They may be asking too much of your time, they may try to humiliate you in front of others, they may criticise you, or they may invade your personal space. To put it simply, they do not respect the boundaries you need to make your life easier.

Ultimately, you may need to ask yourself, 'Who do I need to see less of?' It may be difficult to see less of some people. You may need to be more assertive with certain people. Some people are put off by being assertive because they think being assertive is aggressive.

However, there is a big difference between assertiveness and aggressiveness. Basically, you need to think that both people are right. For example, you are right to refuse a request and the other person is right to make the request. Once you feel you are within your right to say no, your body language follows. If your refusals are just verbal words and deep down you think you are wrong to say no, your body language will indicate this uncertainty and it will be read by the other person as a signal to keep pushing. The assertiveness infographic overleaf will help you to see the differences.

It may also be useful to try to understand why someone is behaving in a certain way that drains you. Try to list their behaviours that drain you, for example, always being late, always being critical (remember that perfectionists tend to be self-critical), or getting easily frustrated, etc. It becomes easier to manage if you can separate the behaviour from the person.

You still have the right to reduce contact and say no but trying to understand the behaviour, instead of getting frustrated and upset and labelling that person in your mind, could be less exhausting for you. Also, once you can explain someone's behaviour you can become better at predicting that behaviour, which then becomes less uncertain and again less exhausting. It is also useful to visualise a barrier between you and the draining person. See their behaviours and comments landing at the barrier and bouncing back to them. Tell yourself, 'I will not let that comment in.' It can also be useful to visualise yourself grabbing a hurtful comment before it lands at your barrier and then throwing it back to the draining person.

It is also useful to think about your limits with people. What behaviours are unacceptable for you? What behaviours makes you feel that someone else is controlling you? Make a list, look at the assertiveness infographic, and write a plan for how you will signal that a line has been crossed for you. You may be surprised, on reflection, just how often that line has been crossed in the past. Now is the time to step in and make the necessary changes.

Who you consider 'difficult' is your own personal perception. Understanding your own personality, preferences and triggers may help you recognise the types of people and situations that cause difficulties for you.

GENERAL   BELIEFS

PASSIVE
- Compliant.
- Submissive.
- Talks little.
- Vague, non- committal communication.
- Puts self down, praises others.
- **"I don't mind...that's fine...yes alright."**

YOU'RE OKAY, I'M NOT
Has no opinion, other peoples are always more important so it doesn't matter what they think anyway.

ASSERTIVE
- Actions & expressions fit with words spoken.
- Firm but polite & clear messages.
- Respectful of self and others.
- **"That's a good idea, and how don't we..." or "I can see that, but I'd really like..."**

I'M OKAY, YOU'RE OKAY
Believes all individuals involved are equal and deserving of respect, none more entitled than the other.

AGGRESSIVE
- Sarcastic.
- Always right & knows it all.
- Interrupts & talks over others.
- Critical, patronising & disrespectful of others.
- **"This is what we're doing, if you don't like it, tough."**

I'M OKAY, YOU'RE NOT
Believe they are entitled to have things done their way because they are right and others are less important.

BODY

EYES
Avoids eye contact, looks down, teary, pleading.
POSTURE
Makes body smaller – stooped, leaning, hunched shoulders.
HANDS
Together, fidgety, clammy.

EYES
Warm, welcoming, friendly, comfortable eye contact.
POSTURE
Relaxed, open, welcoming.
HANDS
Open, friendly & appropriate gestures.

EYES
Narrow, emotionless, staring, and expressionless.
POSTURE
Makes body bigger – upright, head high, feet apart.
HANDS
Pointing fingers, clenched fists, hands on hips.

CONSEQUENCES

Give in to others, don't get what we want or need, self-critical and miserable

Good relationships with others, happy with outcome and to compromise.

Make enemies, upset others and self, feel angry and resentful.

COMMON TYPES OF DIFFICULT PEOPLE:

- Controlling people.

- Intimidating people.

- Passive/passive-aggressive people.

- Unpredictable people.

- Pessimistic people.

- Perfectionists.

- Know-it-all's.

- Show-offs.

- Gossips.

DEALING WITH ANXIETY AND WORRY

Working to decrease your anxiety can help you to cope with your fatigue in several ways. Anxiety is an unpleasant sensation and by tackling it you can work towards improving your mood. This will help you to cope better with the challenges you face as a result of your fatigue. Anxiety is notorious for being a mental condition, but it can also have a physical impact on you. Anxiety can absorb a lot of your energy that could be better used elsewhere and can wreak havoc with your all-important sleep patterns. So, you can see that dealing with anxiety is a key component of coping with fatigue.

In this section, I have two practical strategies to help you deal with your anxiety and to allow you to move towards a calmer and more peaceful mindset. These are the worry tree and circles of control and influence.

THE WORRY TREE FOR PROBLEM-SOLVING

Worrying thoughts are one of the most bothersome symptoms of anxiety. People who are prone to anxiety disorders tend to spend a lot of time focusing on worrying. While you may believe that worrying helps you to avoid and solve problems, the truth is that excessive worrying is unhelpful and a drain on your mental energy, standing in the way of the things you want to do and the person you want to be.

The worry tree gives you a key strategy for coping with worrying thoughts as they arise. The tree differentiates between two common types of worries:

1. **Hypothetical worries** - These occur when we get bogged down in the 'what-ifs' and the 'maybes' and focus on worst-case scenarios. For example, you may have not received a phone call for a while from a loved one, so you begin to wonder if they are seriously ill or have been involved in a terrible accident. This can be followed by intrusive and unwanted worries about what would happen if that really was the situation. These types of worries are often about things completely beyond our control and can lead us to believe that the scenario is more likely than it really is. We get so overwhelmed by the fear of the worst-case scenario, we fail to acknowledge the logic of the actual situation. If we were to

take a step back and observe the situation analytically, then we may understand there is little to get worried about.

2. **Current worries** - These worries, on the other hand, relate to real problems that are happening now. These are within our control to influence. The worry tree gives you ways of dealing with the problem instead of simply worrying about it, helping you to regain a sense of control and therefore reducing anxiety.

The worry tree breaks down the problem-solving process into the following steps:

ACKNOWLEDGING YOUR WORRY

The first step is to notice that you are worrying and to clearly determine what you are worried about. For example, you may be worrying about a difficult financial situation or concerned that your bus is late and that you may be in trouble with your boss. Try to decide whether this is a current problem (the financial situation) or a hypothetical situation (being late and being fired). Also, ask yourself whether there is anything you can practically do to influence either situation.

IF YOU DECIDE YOUR CONCERN IS HYPOTHETICAL:

If your worry is hypothetical, then this means there is very little you can do about the situation. You can either choose to let go of your feelings of anxiety or come back to the worry at a later point. Whichever you decide, find something else to focus on to direct your thoughts away from the worry.

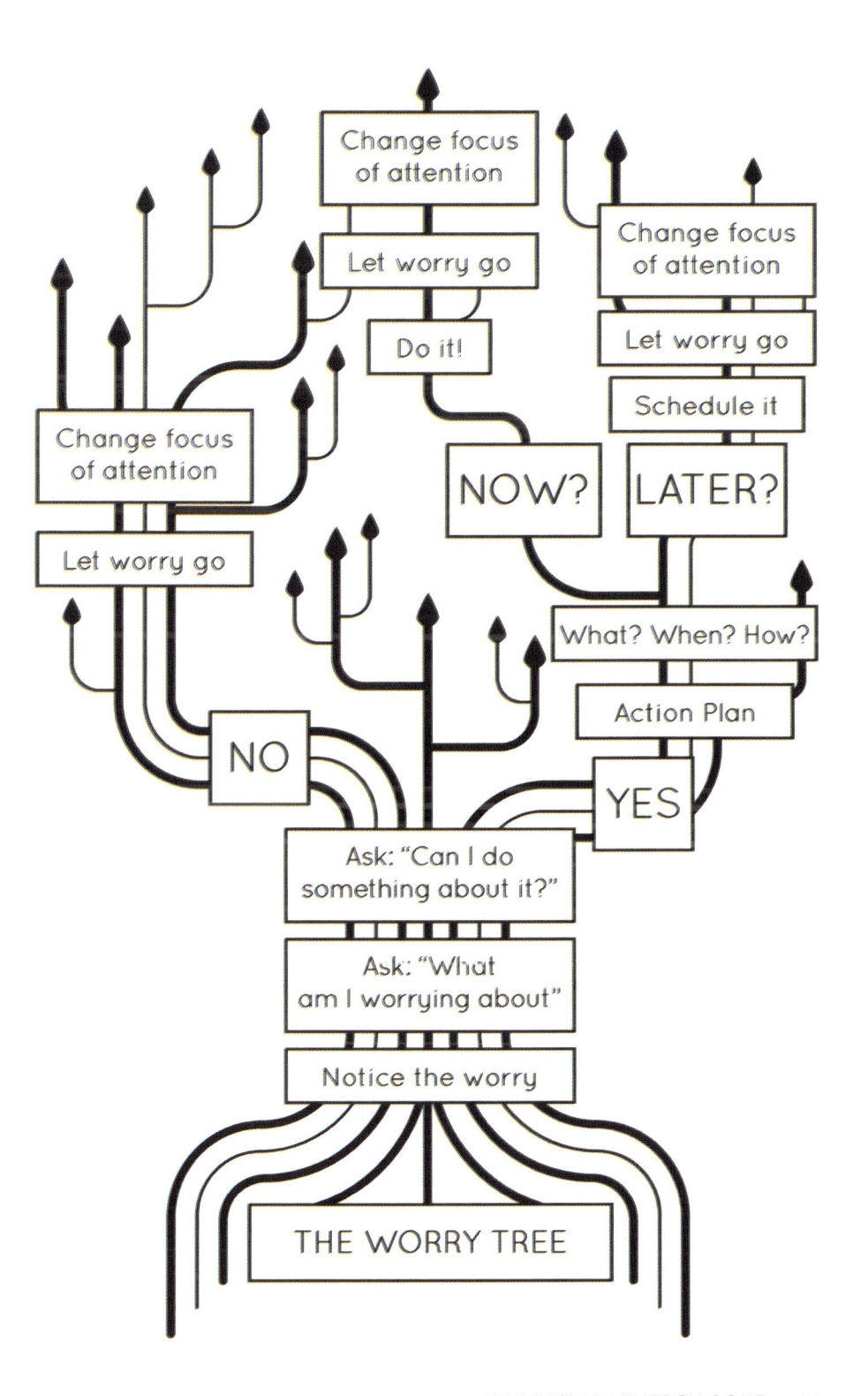

The Worry Tree

- Change focus of attention
- Let worry go

Change focus of attention
Let worry go
Do it!

Change focus of attention
Let worry go
Schedule it

NOW? **LATER?**

Change focus of attention
Let worry go

What? When? How?
Action Plan

NO **YES**

Ask: "Can I do something about it?"

Ask: "What am I worrying about"

Notice the worry

THE WORRY TREE

IF THE WORRY IS A CURRENT ISSUE:

Current problems are those that can be tackled through positive action. Plan how you will tackle the current problem to help alleviate your worry. Brainstorm a range of solutions. Do not think about the effectiveness of the solutions just yet just list possible solutions. Then look at the clearly defined problem and ask yourself whether the proposed solution will help the defined problem. Choose the best solution first and plan a specific time to deal with it. Until that time, let go of your concern and find something else to do to shift your focus away from anxiety. If the first solution does not work, try the next solution.

Letting go of your worry can be easier said than done. If you are suffering from an anxiety disorder or are caught in a cycle of worry, simply releasing yourself from worry can be difficult to do. Try using this helpful mindfulness technique as a strategy developed by Russ Harris to help free yourself from worry over the things you cannot control.

1. Sit in a comfortable position and either close your eyes or rest them gently on a fixed spot in the room.

2. Visualise yourself sitting beside a gently flowing stream with leaves floating along on the surface of the water. Pause for 10 seconds.

3. For the next few minutes, take each thought that enters your mind and place it on a leaf… let it float by. Do this with each thought – pleasurable, painful, or neutral. Even if you have joyous or enthusiastic thoughts, place them on a leaf and let them float by.

4. If your thoughts momentarily stop, continue to watch the stream. Sooner or later, your thoughts will start up again. Pause for 20 seconds.

5. Allow the stream to flow at its own pace. Do not try to speed it up and rush your thoughts along. You are not trying to rush the leaves along or 'get rid' of your worries. You are allowing them to come and go at their own pace.

6. If your mind says, 'This is stupid', 'I'm bored' or 'I'm not doing this right', place those thoughts on leaves too and let them pass. Pause for 20 seconds.

7. If a leaf gets stuck, allow it to hang around until it is ready to float by. If the thought comes up again, watch it float by another time. Pause for 20 seconds.

8. If a difficult or painful feeling arises, simply acknowledge it. Say to yourself, 'I notice myself having a feeling of boredom/impatience/frustration.' Place those thoughts on leaves and allow them to float along.

9. From time to time, your thoughts may hook you and distract you from being fully present in this exercise. This is normal. As soon as you realise that you have become side-tracked, gently bring your attention back to the visualisation exercise.

If you are used to routinely worrying, especially about things outside your control, letting go of your worries may not come naturally. Do not beat yourself up for that. It can be difficult to break yourself out of a pattern that has ruled you for much of your waking life. But do not give up. By using this exercise on a regular basis, you will eventually come to terms with letting go of worry and the process will become gradually easier. Every time you practise it, it gets a little easier. But you have to detach yourself frequently. That is the hard part. But it gets easier. As you do the exercise, focus on how the worry makes you feel. Worrying is unpleasant and the feelings associated with it will almost always be negative. Placing these feelings on a leaf and sending them away too, replaces them with a more energetic feeling.

Tackling over-worrying is really worth your while, especially if you suffer from fatigue and associated muscle tension. Studies have found that the more anxious and stressed people are, the more tense and constricted their muscles become. However, excessive stress or worry can make it worse. As you start to let go of your worries, I suggest you focus on your muscles. What happens to your body as you let go of your worry and stress?

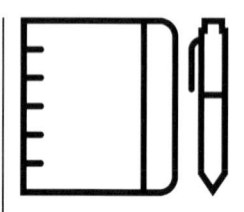

Circles of control and influence.

Understanding the difference between control and influence helps you to differentiate between situations and problems that you can control and ones that you have no reasonable way of influencing.

Draw three circles. Think about a situation that is bothering you.

Label the first circle Control. Write inside the circle all the factors that you can control. There are relatively few things that we have direct control over. These are things such as our daily activities, when we go to bed, and what to eat for dinner, for example.

Label the second circle Influence. Although we do not have direct control over the problems or situations that fall in this circle, we can influence them in some way with our actions. However, we cannot control them entirely. These could be things such as how our child achieves at school, what people think of us, or whether we are promoted at work.

Label the third circle No Control. You should be able to fill this circle. This might include wider factors, such as the weather, transport delays, or what is happening in the news. While we may worry about these scenarios, there is no practical action that we can take to control them one way or the other.

The circles of control and influence are useful for helping us to decide whether something is worth expending our energy on. Try categorising your current concern into the circle where it fits best. If it falls into the circle of control, this is a situation you have direct control over. If the worry falls into the circle of influence, there may be something you can do to affect the outcome one way or the other. You will need to decide whether this is realistic and whether it is worth expending your energy on. If it is, you can make an action plan. If not, try to let go of the worry or postpone thinking about it to another time. Worries falling into the circle of no control may seem very concerning, but it is important to accept that this is something you cannot control. When you find yourself worrying about these types of issues, try to refocus your mental energy elsewhere.

TAKE STEPS TO NOURISH YOUR BODY

Committing to a lifestyle that values nourishing your body is important for burnout prevention. It also helps to plan how you will take care of your body if you need to temporarily step outside your optimum zone, such as to meet a tight deadline. The body and brain can cope with these temporary stresses. The more you commit to taking care of yourself during such a moment, the more resilience you will build up and the less likely you are to wear out your body.

Make sure your brain does not dry out. A 2% decrease in hydration can lead to a 20% loss in energy and the ability to think correctly.

Our bodies all require water. If you do not like water, add some flavour. Try some vegetable or fruit slices, or herbs, such as mint or basil. Remember, good nutrition is also important for concentration and cognitive fitness.

If you like cold water, do you have enough available? Think about buying a jug or bottle for the fridge.

Are you in the habit of taking water with you when you leave your home? If not, what do you need to do to make this a habit? What reminders do you need to make this a new habit? It can be quite confusing to know what healthy eating is. We have an overload of information, gadgets and apps about healthy eating. Trying to keep up with what is 'good' and 'bad' food can be mentally draining. It can make you over-think and over worry about food, leading to draining emotions, such as guilt, fear and anxiety.

It can also lead to eating habits that are physically draining as certain food groups are omitted or restricted. A healthy principle for energised eating is quite simple; eat a range of good food types when you are hungry. The problem is we interfere with the process of eating far too much. We eat too much because we are exhausted and because we use food to avoid our negative emotions. We eat because an app has beeped and told us it is time to eat.

I will never forget a client who became obsessed with a fitness app. She was constantly stressing about what to eat and not eat and when to eat. She often found herself reaching for snacks then feeling guilty, keeping her in a cycle of low self-esteem, restriction of food and then over-eating. She felt completely exhausted to be in this cycle of self and body monitoring. I suggested she ditched the app. Her reply was, "But how will I know when I'm hungry?" In a short space of time, the number of people who have become so out of touch with trusting their own signals for hunger has increased. They have started to become too reliant on external cues to tell them what and when to eat. My suggestion to you is to get back to some basics.

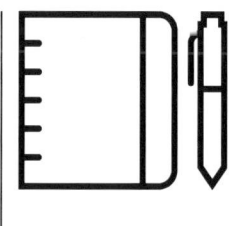

I want you to pause after you have eaten and ask yourself, 'How does my body feel?' Make a note in your notebook of the foods that make you feel heavy. Be careful to focus on the physical sensations, not your thoughts, such as:

'I feel so bad, I shouldn't have eaten that.'

'I'm going to get so fat now.'

'Why did I eat that?'

Attune yourself to your bodily feelings.

Does the food make your body feel heavy? Do you feel lightheaded? Do you feel energised? Do you feel sick? Do you get a headache? Does your stomach feel irritated? Does any other part of your body feel irritated? In doing this exercise, you will learn to know which foods work for you and to notice and trust when your body needs food.

Your brain uses 20% of the energy produced by your body. If your energy supply is too low, you risk experiencing a range of symptoms, including memory problems, fatigue and concentration problems. A healthy diet can support your brain's function as the brain requires certain types of fuel every day. Your brain also needs certain nutrients to keep it working at its optimum level.

The best foods for executive brain function, when eaten as part of a balanced diet, include:

- Oily fish.

- Dark chocolate.

- Berries.

- Nuts and seeds.

- Whole grains.

- Avocados.

- Eggs.

- Oranges.

- Turmeric.

- Lentils and black beans.

- Vegetables.

- Leafy greens.

- Soy products.

- Wholegrain foods.

By choosing to eat these types of foods, you can help maintain your brain's health as well as boost your alertness, memory and mood.

CREATE A 'TO DO' LIST FOR YOUR DISTRACTION

We live in a world where we can have access to information instantly. We can have an answer to a question in our hands within seconds of thinking it. As a result, many people toggle away from what they are working on the instant a thought about needing more information pops into their mind. The problem with this is that once you are distracted, it takes an average of 25 minutes to return to the original task. Also, shifting your attention back and forth drains your brain, as the shifting itself requires energy.

To stay focused, whenever something pops into your head, write it down on a piece of paper next to you or on an electronic note. Tell yourself you will look at this when you take a break from what it is you are trying to focus on. You can then evaluate the distraction to-do list and ask yourself if it is still worthy of some attention and time.

DEFINE YOUR MODE

We are at our optimum when we are focusing on one task. However, we need to do lots of different types of tasks throughout the day. It is useful to portion your day into categories of time and then only do that category of a task at that particular time. We also have to play lots of different roles in life. Jumping in and out of these roles can be exhausting. I recommend acknowledging which role or mode you are in throughout the day. Then have a little word with yourself and tell yourself to get into this mode. Examples of modes might be: work mode, parent mode, friend mode, partner mode, learning mode, driving mode or relaxing mode. So, as you enter your home after a day at work, you might say to yourself, 'I'm now entering into parent mode.' Within these modes, there are different types of tasks or demands. When you are in work mode, you may need to do a range of different categories of tasks, such as admin, creative, leadership, strategic, physical or organising. Try to organise your tasks so that you limit the amount of switching between different categories of tasks.

DEALING WITH SLEEP PROBLEMS

Sleep problems are commonly experienced alongside fatigue. They can be exacerbated if you are experiencing painful symptoms or are worrying a lot. Also, if you find yourself sleeping for long periods during the day, this can make falling and staying asleep at night very difficult, with those eight hours now being delivered in chunks. However, trying to establish healthy sleeping habits and routines is very important. Disordered routines will make achieving good quality sleep and waking feeling refreshed and re-energised practically impossible. However, by implementing some practical measures, you can take your first steps towards more healthy and energising sleep habits. Here are my top strategies for establishing good sleeping patterns:

1. Try to let go of worries before you go to sleep. If you have anxious thoughts whirling around your brain, it can be near impossible to nod off quickly. So, it is a good idea to try to deal with worries at least an hour before you settle down. Schedule some 'worry time'. Use the worry tree to help you deal with your worries.

2. If you do not have the time to deal with worries before bed, consider jotting down your worries in a notebook and tell yourself you will come back to them in the morning.

3. If you find yourself still thinking before bed, repeat the word

'the' in your head and tell yourself that night-time is for sleep and that the brain is less effective at dealing with worries at night. The word 'the' is a boring and meaningless word that will suppress your unhelpful thoughts.

4. Establish a regular sleep routine. Irregular bedtimes and waking times can make it difficult to sleep through the night. Although it may seem hard, try to go to bed and wake up at the same time every day, including at the weekends. Over time, your body will adjust to this new routine and you will be more likely to feel sleepy at bedtime.

5. Avoid substances that could interfere with your sleep, especially in the afternoons and before bed. These include alcohol, nicotine, and caffeinated beverages and foods.

6. Do not stay in bed if you cannot sleep. You want your body to associate your bed with sleeping so that it is ready to fall asleep when you settle down for bed. For this reason, it is also a good idea not to watch TV or carry out any other activities whilst lying in bed. If you cannot sleep, get up and take part in a calming activity, such as reading for a while, until you feel ready to nod off.

DEALING WITH LOW MOOD AND DEPRESSION

Many people with fatigue develop feelings of depression and low mood. Depression can also affect the way you experience fatigue, making your symptoms more intense. Many people find it difficult to ask for help when dealing with depression, but it is not a sign of weakness at all. In fact, depression is a common mental illness and could strike anybody at any time. It does not denote any kind of lack of strength or determination. If you are struggling with depression, you deserve the help you need to feel better.

Some thinking styles are commonly shared amongst people with depression. Perfectionist style 'all or nothing' thinking, focusing on hypothetical worries and assuming the worst are all common thinking styles when you are suffering from depression. If you recognise these thinking patterns in yourself, it is important to acknowledge and challenge them. With depression can often come deep self-loathing, to the point where even the tiniest, most understandable mistake on your part is all the excuse you need to start doubting yourself and telling yourself you do not deserve to be better.

The 'all or nothing' thinking style is particularly associated with depression. It is the tendency to think in terms of binary oppositions, such as 'good' or 'bad', 'black' or 'white', and 'healthy' or 'unhealthy'. This kind of thinking is quite rigid and can cause frustration and disappointment. Being frustrated and disappointed on a regular basis zaps your energy levels.

Using a thought record can be useful to help you capture and re-evaluate depressive thoughts. Here is an example of how you can start to challenge one of these unhelpful thinking patterns:

Ask yourself:

What is in the middle?

What am I overlooking/not seeing?

If I drew a scale from 0-100, what would be 75?

Dealing with depression requires help, understanding and support from others, and often from trained professionals. Although it may feel hard, it is important to seek the help you need to begin to recover. While this may feel like admitting defeat, seeking support is a brave and courageous step. More and more people are seeking professional help for depression, including very successful people. Depression can creep up on anyone. Remember, you deserve support and compassion to help you get better. Take a moment to think about asking for help.

You can download a Depression Thought Record from my website to make a start with easing your depression.

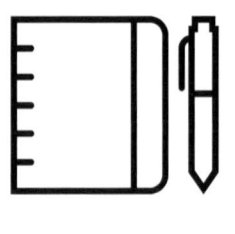

What do you think when you envision yourself asking for help? What do you feel in your body? Re- evaluate your thoughts by asking yourself, 'What would I say to a friend who needed help?'

DEALING WITH FOCUSING ON THE SYMPTOMS IN YOUR BODY

When you think about asking for help, does the feeling in your body give you any clues as to what might be stopping you from seeking help?

Often, we feel stress acutely in our bodies. This can be unpleasant and can also serve to worsen exhaustion symptoms. The way you think about your stressed body can cause further tension and stress. You may be angry with your body or you may feel hopeless, as though if you cannot control your body, you cannot control your situation. That is depression and self-loathing doing the talking.

Here are two techniques to empower you to make peace with your body and start to influence how you experience your stressed body. Experiment with both techniques; you may find you prefer one or like using both in combination.

LET GO

Many of my clients tell me that they don't have time for meditation, mindfulness or guided relaxation. Therefore, I have created a short but powerful technique that, if practised on a regular basis, teaches your body to learn to relax by practising good breathing and muscle relaxation. If you take away only one technique from the book, then I highly recommend this one.

You can download it here -
zenitudeselfhelp.com/cbt-downloads-subscribe

The Let Go audio also helps to activate the parasympathetic nervous system, which is the part of the nervous system that slows your body down. Remember the function of the vagus nerve from Phase 2? Deep breathing alerts the vagus nerve to slow down the stress response. Breathing in activates the sensory nodes on our lungs, sending information through the vagus nerve and into the brain. Breathing out then causes the brain to send information back down through the vagus nerve to slow down or speed up the heart. When your mind judges everything to seem safe, the brain then sends a message down the vagus nerve to lower the heart and breathing rate. You start to feel relaxed and confident. It also works the other way around. If you consciously tell yourself to take a slow, deep breath and relax your muscles, a signal will travel up to the brain and you will begin to feel more in control and confident.

Make peace with your body:

Start by closing your eyes and focusing on how you are feeling. Pause and reflect, what does that sensation need?

- Soften

Once you have found the area of your body where you are experiencing the stress, begin by gently trying to soften the area, relaxing the muscles. If focusing on this area causes you discomfort, focus on your breathing until the sensation passes.

- Soothe

Next, soothe yourself lovingly because you are experiencing stress and discomfort. Direct kind and compassionate thoughts towards yourself and the area in which you are experiencing stress, tension or pain.

- Allow

Finally, allow and accept the discomfort to exist in you. Allow it to come and go naturally. Notice whether your attention is too over-focused on these sensations. If so, remind yourself that you have soothed your body, take a deep breath and change your focus of attention. It is good to think about when you tend to over-focus and pre-plan how you could change your focus of attention.

BODY LANGUAGE AND POSTURE

Body language is conveyed in everything non-verbal that you do; how you move, sit or stand, as well as your expressions and mannerisms. Body language is often communicated instinctively rather than consciously. However, our bodies have the power to influence our minds. In turn, our minds can influence our behaviour, and our behaviour can change our outcomes.

What is your body language saying now? Maybe you are hunched over, perhaps your legs are crossed, or you are wrapping a foot around an ankle. When we feel powerless or exhausted, we close up, wrap our bodies up, make ourselves smaller.

The non-verbal expressions of power and energy are the opposite. They are about expanding. So, instead of wrapping yourself up and making yourself smaller, make yourself big, stretch out, and take up space. It is about allowing yourself to open up and literally stand tall and proud.

In Phase 2 we covered paying attention to how your body feels, but it is important to pay attention to what your body is saying too. Try to become conscious of your own non-verbal language. Become aware of displaying 'small' body language and change your posture to make yourself 'big'. If you do it enough times, you will internalise the new behaviour and take another step towards becoming the version of yourself that you are hoping to transition into.

PACE YOURSELF

We live in a world where achievement is highly valued. Humans need to feel some sort of challenge and mastery; however, it is not our only need. Beyond our basic needs, we also need play and care. Think about your life. Is it too achievement-heavy? Do you have enough fun activities which give you a sense of enjoyment? Do you take enough care of yourself? What about activities that motivate and energise you? Engaging in a regular energising activity will improve your mood and help you use the energy created by the adrenaline response if you are feeling stressed, anxious or angry.

Decide what you need to do to pace your life and create more balance in the types of activities that you do. Be realistic. Start with a small change. Think about when you can do these other activities, how you can do them, what preparation you need to do, and who you will do them with. Then take some time to schedule an activity that is more playful and caring.

Then, notice how the activity affects you. If it turns out to be unhelpful then ask yourself if you could have done anything differently. It is fine if you decide not to do it again because it is not for you. Ask yourself what the next activity you want to experiment with is. If it has a helpful or positive effect, then plan your next step to do more. Give time to schedule these activities as much priority as your achievement-related activities.

DIGITAL DETOX

Digital detox, where you refrain from using smartphones, computers and social media platforms, is a well-known way of dealing with the over-use of technology. People report sleeping better and feeling like they have more time when they choose to switch off their devices. Yet many people are reluctant to take time away from their devices because they fear it will be overwhelming to return to a barrage of demands and information when they return to their devices. However, the opposite is often true. After a digital detox, people report coming back to their devices with a new perspective of what is important and are more able to define what is urgent.

If you plan a digital detox, accept that you will feel uneasy at first but do not let this put you off. Define how long you want the digital detox to be. The time-frame is personal to you and your life. Even making the choice to switch off your phone for one hour during the day can be beneficial. Try to plan something pleasurable when you choose your detox time. If you can, try to spend some time in nature with your phone switched off. It helps to restore focus and attention. It is often a time when you suddenly have a good idea, or you make a decision.

As well as a fixed period for a digital detox, it is good to set boundaries around your phone use. Here are some tips:

- Designate an area of the home that devices are off-limits. I think a basic one should be at the table.

- Turn off the Wi-Fi at a certain time of the day, such as an hour before bed, and leave it off all night.

- Designate an area for charging phones, this helps to signal that phones have a place in your life and are not permitted into all areas of your life.

- If there are any apps that you want to reduce usage, put them in a folder on your phone. This one extra step of opening the app can make the action more deliberate.

- Try to avoid looking at news broadcasts or notifications. If we see a message or a news report, we are either taking in the information or trying to work out how we should be replying to it. Have a cut-off point for these kinds of notifications. They have no place in a peaceful mindset.

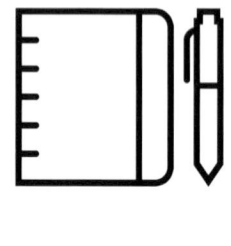

You should now have some insights into what factors are contributing to your exhaustion and how you can make changes. It is time to plan your next steps, dealing with one factor at a time. However, before you start to make changes, think about what obstacles may prevent you from making the change, then brainstorm how you would overcome the obstacle.

For example, you may recognise that you are too tired to cook healthy meals. What solutions are available to you? Write down as many ideas as possible then choose the best solution for you. To continue with the example, you could plan some quick, easy, healthy options. It may mean changing what you consider to be healthy. It may mean taking it in turns to batch cook with a friend. It may mean buying more frozen vegetables rather than fresh vegetables. It may mean preparing breakfast the night before. It may mean asking someone in the family to regularly chop up fruit and keep it in the fridge.

Now it is time to start planning and implementing your goals for change. Once you have a list of what you would like to change, start to add some realistic time-frames for change. I must remind you again, please don't be tempted to try to fix everything at once. It is highly likely that you will create further anxiety and fatigue.

Here is an example of a plan for change.

I've noticed the following contributing factors to burnout, that I'd like to change:

1. I engage in too much 'all or nothing' thinking.

2. I worry too much.

3. I try too hard to please difficult people.

Re-read the sections on dealing with the above contributing factors to burnout.

Rate how doable each suggestion is for you on a scale of 1-5, with 1 being not very doable and 5 being doable. Start with the most doable then, set a time-frame to help you keep focused on the change, then move to the next goal of change.

For example:

- **Week 1 - 2**
  I'm going to become more mindful of 'all or nothing' thinking and start to ask myself, 'What's in the middle?'

- **Week 3 - 5**
  I'm going to use the worry tree at the end of each day for three weeks.

- **Week 6 - 10**
  I'm going to practise more assertive communication with person X.

When you have worked through Phase 3, take a little time to look back over your progress and congratulate yourself on your successes.

You have turned a major corner and have done most of the legwork needed to start living in your optimum zone. It is one thing to start a new habit, it is another keeping it. We do not allow ourselves enough time for private reflection periods, which is why when we decide we want to make changes, we never know how to go about it or even what to change. So, feel free to revisit this section as often as necessary whenever you feel like you need some guidance. The next chapter will help you keep on track regarding the optimum zone.

PHASE 4

Living in your Optimum Zone

AFTER YOU HAVE EXPERIMENTED AND MADE SOME changes, it is time to stay in your optimum zone. Of course, there will be times when you slip out of it - that is life. The key to staying in your optimum zone is to be aware that you have slipped out of it and to make a plan to get back into it. If you know when you will be able to get back into your optimum zone, it is empowering. If you feel empowered, your body does not need its full stress response because it has registered the temporary nature and you have signalled that you can cope. There is no lingering danger that your body needs to protect you from.

If you are aware that you have slipped, you can take small steps to protect yourself when you are out of your optimum zone. For example, if you know you are in a busy period, you could make a decision to have an energising juice instead of that second coffee. You could take the time to walk part of the way home after work and clear your head before you enter the demands of the home. You could commit to using the time you do have to make a nourishing meal. Knowing you have slipped out of your optimum zone helps you to make deliberate actions to protect yourself.

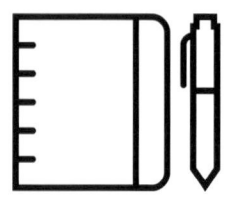

It is good to think about your early warning signs for slipping out of your optimum zone.

- How do you know you have slipped out of your optimum zone? What starts to happen? How do you start to feel?

- What do you start to do when you have slipped out of this zone?

- What do you need to do if you slip outside of your optimum zone?

- What do you need to stop doing if you slip outside of your optimum zone?

- Whose help do you need?

- What do you need to remember?

- How will you help yourself to remember what you need when you slip out of your optimum zone?

Finally, consider your personal qualities that will help you when you slip out of your optimum zone. You are a unique individual with a unique set of strengths that you can draw upon as you work towards your new positive future. Perhaps you are resilient, kind, or a good communicator? Make a list of the strengths you have in your tool-kit that will allow you to ensure you stay in your optimum zone for longer. Sometimes, it can be hard to see and recognise positive qualities in yourself. You may want to ask a trusted loved one who knows you well to help you with this exercise.

Look at the box of examples below to help you define your strengths. Which strengths do you need to draw upon to continue to make progress?

Sincere	Wise	Thoughtful
Calm	Organised	Creative
Patient	Positive	Generous
Determined	Dependable	Resilient
Appreciative	Engaging	Insightful
Warm	Humorous	Caring
Focused	Brave	Fair
Strategic	Rigorous	Independent
Understanding	Detailed	Hopeful
Open-minded	Practical	Playful
Curious	Supportive	Decisive

FINALLY

BY COMPLETING THE PROCESSES IN THIS BOOK, YOU have taken great steps towards a more positive, optimised future. Changing deeply ingrained habits and ways of thinking is never easy, but I believe the effort will pay dividends in giving you back energy. As discussed, modern life can be difficult, demanding and distracting. That aside, we are living in amazing times with many opportunities to learn, grow and connect. Technological advancements can improve our lives in so many ways, however, we must be in control of technologies, rather than let technology control what we do with our time. We must make conscious choices and take deliberate actions in our use of new technologies. If not, they become another way to feel powerless and disconnected.

I hope this book has convinced you that you have the power and ability to make choices. I know it is not easy, but it does not need to be made harder by the things we think, do, or tell ourselves. In moving forward, I would like you to accept that change is an accumulative process. I see change as a series of micro-movements in behaviours, thoughts, emotions, body sensations and body posture. It is important to commit to the long journey of change and to acknowledge and celebrate the small changes that you do make.

I also hope that you have learnt that being busy all the time is not glamorous or prestigious, nor does it make you more productive. When you consider the effort needed to stay in your optimum zone, staying busy all the time is actually easier than taking the time to pursue a life that you value and gives you purpose and energy. Good things in life often take time and effort.

Revisit this book as often as you need to. Whenever you feel you are stumbling out of your optimum zone, please come back to the phases and work through them again:

- **Phase 1:**
  Motivation and seeing the end in your mind.

- **Phase 2:**
  Understanding WHY you are exhausted.

- **Phase 3:**
  Making changes to stay within your optimum zone.

- **Phase 4:**
  Living in your optimum zone.

Your life is your story. You are the author of your own story. You can choose to take positive steps forward and leave behind the herd of people who are normalising being exhausted. 'I'm so tired' or 'I'm exhausted' does not have to be your story too. I hope you can trust that feeling exhausted all the time is your body trying to talk to you, to warn you that there is a problem.

Listen to it before it tries harder to get your attention.

Remember to take time to be kind and compassionate towards yourself, and to congratulate yourself on all the steps you do take towards making your life more energised and fulfilling.

I wish you all the serenity and happiness that comes with feeling stronger, more energised, and in full control of your life.

ADDITIONAL RESOURCES

Free Test of Your Attention and Mental Concentration Abilities.

You can use the test in the link below to start to understand how burnout may be impacting your cognitive abilities. The test is fun and quick to use, it has been developed by scientists at Cambridge University, UK. Once you start to make some changes, you can go back to the test to see if the changes you are making are improving your Attention and Mental Concentration.

Visit -
tinyurl.com/ZenAttention

Free hypnosis download to help you focus and concentrate.

Visit -
tinyurl.com/ZenitudeHyp

ZENitude Self Help

All of the illustrations and material in this book are available at ZENitudeselfhelp.com.

Find out more about booking a one-to-one therapy or online coaching session at ZENitudeselfhelp.com.

Recommended Books

You will find a list of recommended books in the link below:

www.zenitudeselfhelp.com/books-1

Instagram

Receive Regular Inspiration from my Instagram Page:

@zenitudeselfhelp

YouTube

I recommend that you watch these videos, which explain in more detail the allostatic load which, in a nutshell, is a measure of 'wear and tear' on the body:

tinyurl.com/Zenwearout

tinyurl.com/Zenwearout2

I recommend watching Amy Cuddy talk about how your body language can shape you:

tinyurl.com/ZenAmyC

Printed in Great Britain
by Amazon